Machine Unlearning

This book explores one of the most critical and emerging fields in artificial intelligence (AI): machine unlearning. As data privacy concerns grow and regulations like GDPR (General Data Protection Regulation) demand compliance, this book provides a comprehensive guide to selectively removing learned information from machine learning models without sacrificing performance or requiring complete retraining. Covering foundational principles, advanced algorithms, benchmarking tools, and real-world case studies in healthcare, finance, and social media, the book bridges the gap between theory and practice. It also addresses ethical, legal, and societal implications, offering insights into creating trustworthy AI systems. This book is an essential resource for understanding and implementing machine unlearning in the era of responsible AI.

Machine Unlearning

Principles, Methods, and Evolving Frontiers

Bitan Misra, Sayan Chakraborty,
and Nilanjan Dey

CRC Press
Taylor & Francis Group
Boca Raton London

CRC Press is an imprint of the
Taylor & Francis Group, an **informa** business

Designed cover image: Shutterstock (Image ID: 2418658999)

First edition published 2027
by CRC Press
2385 NW Executive Center Drive, Suite 320, Boca Raton FL 33431

and by CRC Press
4 Park Square, Milton Park, Abingdon, Oxon, OX14 4RN

CRC Press is an imprint of Taylor & Francis Group, LLC

ISBN: 978-1-041-29531-0 (hbk)
ISBN: 978-1-041-29822-9 (pbk)
ISBN: 978-1-003-77147-0 (ebk)

DOI: 10.1201/9781003771470

Typeset in Times
by Apex CoVantage, LLC

Contents

Author Biographies

Bitan Misra is currently working as an assistant professor in the Department of Computer Science and Engineering, Techno International New Town, Kolkata, India. She received a B. Tech. and M. Tech. dual degree in electronics and telecommunication engineering from KIIT University, Bhubaneswar, India, in 2018. She received a Ph.D. in 2022 from the National Institute of Technology, Durgapur, India. She has published almost 40 research papers in various international journals and conferences and is the author of five books. Her main research interests include optimization techniques, deep learning, evolutionary algorithms, and soft computing techniques. She has worked as a reviewer in several national and international journals and conferences. She is an associate editor of *International Journal of Ambient Computing and Intelligence*. She is a member of IEEE and Internet Society.

Sayan Chakraborty (senior member, IEEE) is currently working as an assistant professor in the Department of Computer Science and Technology at JIS College of Engineering, Kalyani, West Bengal, India. He completed a Ph.D. in image registration from Sikkim Manipal University in 2023. He obtained an M. Tech. degree in computer science and engineering from JIS College of Engineering and obtained a B. Tech. degree from the same institution. He has over 12 years of academic experience. His research interests include digital image processing, nature-inspired algorithms, and machine learning. He has published 92 research papers in international journals, book chapters, and conference proceedings on topics including optimization, artificial intelligence, pattern recognition, and digital image processing. Dr. Chakraborty has authored and edited four books published by Springer, Academia Press, and CRC Press. He is currently serving as an associate editor of the *International Journal of Ambient Computing and Intelligence* and is an Editorial Board member of the *International Journal of Rough Sets and Data Analysis*.

Nilanjan Dey (senior member, IEEE) received B. Tech. and M. Tech. degrees in information technology from West Bengal Board of Technical University and a Ph.D. in electronics and telecommunication engineering from Jadavpur University, Kolkata, India, in 2005, 2011, and 2015. Currently, he is a professor with Techno International New Town, Kolkata, and a visiting fellow of the University of Reading, UK. He is the Editor-in-Chief of the *International Journal of Ambient Computing and Intelligence*, Associate Editor of *IEEE Transactions on Technology and Society*, and series Co-Editor of *Springer Tracts in Nature-Inspired Computing and Data-Intensive Research* and *Advances in Ubiquitous Sensing Applications for Healthcare*. He is on the Editorial Board of *IEEE Data Descriptions*. He is a fellow of Institution of Electronics and Telecommunication Engineers and member of Institution of Engineers and Internet Society.

Preface

In a world where machine learning models are used more frequently to run real-world systems, erasing particular data in trained models has become a priority, whether it is out of necessity to meet privacy requirements, ethical responsibility, or social justice. As data privacy becomes a prominent concern and regulatory need (i.e., the GDPR), machine unlearning has become a major focus of academia and business. This book highlights the major principles, reasons, and methods of machine unlearning, which is an emerging and crucial field of artificial intelligence (AI) centered on the process of removing learned information in models selectively. It attempts to meet the increasing needs of data confidentiality, ethical AI design, and other regulations by postulating the motivations, principles, and systems that allow systems to forget particular data efficiently. The book defines the concept of gaps between theoretical knowledge and practical application, which allows the reader to find a clear route between known facts and performance in unlearning.

The book addresses the essential principles, technical frameworks, performance criteria, and practical aspects of machine unlearning systematically. Chapter 1 lays the foundation for understanding machine unlearning. Chapter 2 explores the various technical methods used to remove learned data from machine learning models. Chapter 3 focuses on how machine unlearning is applied in the context of generative AI and large language models. Chapter 4 covers how machine unlearning techniques are tested and evaluated. It introduces widely used public datasets and specialized benchmarks created specifically for unlearning research. Chapter 5 presents real-world examples of how machine unlearning is being applied across different industries. Chapter 6 explores the ethical and legal dimensions of machine unlearning. Chapter 7 looks at the key challenges that researchers and developers face when trying to implement machine unlearning effectively. Chapter 8 summarizes the importance of machine unlearning in today's data-driven world, especially for protecting privacy, meeting legal standards, and building trustworthy AI systems. The book highlights emerging issues and future studies and may be used as a guide to students, researchers, and practitioners. The book is created to be readily understandable and followed by professionals to understand the next stage of responsible AI, namely, machine unlearning.

Bitan Misra
Sayan Chakraborty
Nilanjan Dey

1 Introduction to Machine Unlearning

1.1 INTRODUCTION TO MACHINE UNLEARNING

In the recent years, the rapid growth of data and computing power has led to the wide use of machine learning (ML) models across many fields. From healthcare to finance, ML now plays a key role in making decisions and predicting outcomes. Over the past decade, the combination of massive data availability and higher processing power has pushed ML development at an impressive pace. Today, ML algorithms and artificial intelligence (AI) are everyday tools, including on mobile apps and wearable devices. This expansion has led to major progress in areas such as image recognition, language understanding, and recommendation systems, deeply influencing how we live and work. However, as data and user needs constantly evolve, ML models that are fixed after training often fall short and lose effectiveness. With major advances in data storage and transmission, the amount of digital data being created and used has skyrocketed. For example, more than four billion YouTube videos are watched each day [1]. This vast amount of online personal data—digital footprints showing how people behave, interact, and communicate—comes from things such as reviews, blog posts (such as on Medium), social media updates (such as Instagram), and contributions to shared platforms (such as Wikipedia). In many ML systems, data from millions or billions of users are used during training. While this helps improve ML and AI technologies, it also raises serious concerns about privacy and highlights the urgent need for strong data management to protect user information.

The growing use of machine learning has sparked serious concerns about privacy, security, and how well these systems perform in changing environments. ML models are trained using data shared by users, but this can unintentionally lead to privacy risks—because models may remember and expose private user information. This information can potentially be leaked through attacks such as membership inference, property inference, and profiling, even if newer threats have not yet been discovered. Many companies and organizations rely on user data to train ML models for various purposes, from recommending movies to providing healthcare solutions [2]. While some organizations let users withdraw consent and delete their data, others may quietly keep it without permission.

To protect users, governments around the world have introduced data privacy laws that require companies to erase personal data if a user asks. These include the European Union's GDPR (General Data Protection Regulation), California's CCPA (California Consumer Privacy Act), and Canada's proposed CPPA [1–3]. These laws require companies to take real action to remove personal data when requested. In a significant case, the U.S. Federal Trade Commission recently ordered a company to delete not only user data but also any machine learning models and algorithms

DOI: 10.1201/9781003771470-1

built from those data. This decision reinforces the idea that individuals have the right to request the removal of both their personal data and their impact on trained models—not only deleting it from databases but also erasing its influence from the system altogether.

However, retraining machine learning models from scratch every time a user requests their data to be deleted is highly impractical—it can take weeks and cost millions of computing resources. A smarter approach would be to find ways to remove only the specific data points from the model without having to restart the training process. In machine learning, simply deleting the raw training data from databases is not enough to meet the "right to be forgotten" (RTBF) rules. This is because the model may still hold on to patterns or features it learned from the deleted data, either directly or indirectly [4, 5]. These traces can still be targeted by privacy attacks, making full removal more complicated than just clearing a record from storage.

1.2 POTENTIAL APPROACHES

As AI systems become more advanced—the ability to generate, transform, and replicate data—our traditional ideas of privacy, such as the "right to be forgotten," are no longer enough. Simply deleting a post or file does not guarantee true erasure if that data have already influenced an ML model [6, 7]. Privacy needs to be rethought to fit this new reality. Some promising, although not perfect, strategies to help align AI development with personal privacy rights are as follows:

Federated learning

Instead of collecting all user data in one place, federated learning trains models directly on users' devices. In this way, sensitive data remain on the device and never enter a central server. However, this method is technically challenging—it requires high computing power and fast network speeds to train models across many devices at once.

Differential privacy

This technique helps keep data private by adding random noise to the dataset. This makes it very difficult to identify any one person's information while still allowing for useful overall insights. The downside is that the added noise can reduce the model's accuracy; thus, there is a trade-off between privacy and performance.

Machine unlearning (MU) or algorithmic destruction

Instead of retraining the entire model when some data need to be removed, machines unlearn targets and erase only the specific data and their impact. While this is a promising solution, there is currently no standard way to measure its effectiveness. For large, complex models, fully "forgetting" data remains a major challenge.

Recently, machine unlearning has gained attention as a better way to meet privacy regulations such as the right to be forgotten. Unlike traditional deletion methods, which only remove data from storage, the MU changes the model itself—removing any trace of the deleted data so that it behaves as if the data were never used in

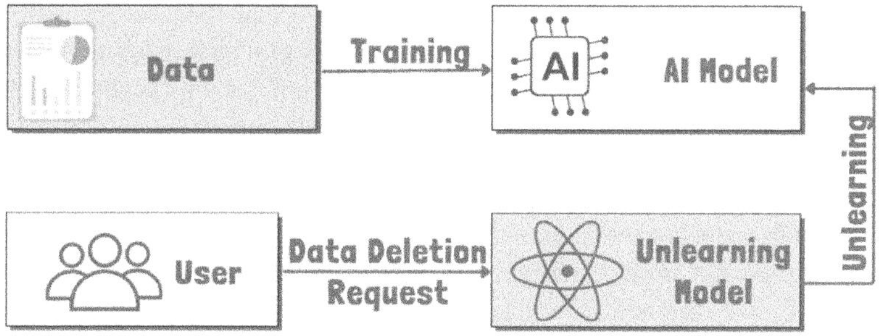

FIGURE 1.1 Machine unlearning.

training. This helps maintain model performance while ensuring compliance with privacy laws. Beyond legal requirements, MUs can also make AI systems more ethical and fair. For example, large language models (LLMs) often learn from vast amounts of internet data, which may contain biased or inappropriate content [7, 8]. MUs can help eliminate these harmful influences, making the models more balanced and trustworthy. It can also remove corrupted or outdated data, which improves both the accuracy and the reliability of the model.

Figure 1.1 shows how machine unlearning works in a simple way. The idea is to make an AI model "forget" certain user data when someone asks for it to be deleted. Instead of retraining the whole model from scratch, unlearning attempts to reverse the effect that the specific data have on the model. Since every piece of data slightly changes how the model behaves, unlearning focuses on identifying and removing just those changes—like hitting the undo button for that data—so it is as if the model never saw it in the first place.

1.3 MOTIVATION FOR UNLEARNING

Individuals might want their data to be deleted from an AI system for many reasons. These reasons generally fall into four categories: security, privacy, usability, and fidelity. Here, there is a simple explanation of each:

Security

AI models, especially deep learning systems, can be tricked by "adversarial attacks." These attacks use data that look almost identical to real input but are designed to confuse the model and make it give wrong answers. In sensitive areas such as healthcare, an incorrect prediction could lead to a misdiagnosis or the wrong treatment. Therefore, when such harmful data are detected, it becomes important to remove them quickly via machine unlearning to ensure that the system is safe.

Privacy

Privacy laws such as the GDPR in Europe and the CCPA in California give people the right to have their personal data deleted. This right has become more important because of real privacy concerns—such as leaks from cloud services, which may store multiple copies of data across different servers or backups. There have also been cases in which machine learning systems accidentally revealed private information, such as genetic markers in healthcare data. Because of such risks, users may want to delete their data to protect their privacy.

Usability

People often use recommendation systems in apps and online services. If these systems do not properly forget bad or incorrect data—such as mistakes, spam, or out-of-place searches—they can keep making poor suggestions. For example, if someone accidentally searches for an illegal item, they might continue seeing recommendations for it across different devices, even after their browsing history is clear. This kind of bad user experience can frustrate people and lead them to stop using the service.

Fidelity (Fairness)

Sometimes, users ask for their data to be removed because the model is biased. Even with recent improvements, AI can still show unfair behavior. For example, a tool called COMPAS, which is used in courtrooms, was found to give African American individuals higher risk scores than white individuals do, despite not using race as an input. Other examples include AI used in beauty contests that show bias against darker skin tones or facial recognition systems struggling with certain ethnic features. In such cases, unlearning can help remove the data or patterns that cause biased or unfair outcomes.

Bias in AI often comes from the data used to train the models. For example, if an AI system is trained mostly on images of white people—like those found in popular datasets such as ImageNet—it may struggle to accurately process images of black individuals. Similarly, in job application screening, the model might unintentionally learn to associate certain outcomes with gender or race, even if these features are not included. To address such issues, it is important to "unlearn" the biased data and the patterns from which the model is selected.

To do this well, a good machine unlearning (MU) algorithm should meet three key criteria:

Effectiveness

The model should forget all the information related to the data being removed—as if it had never seen it. While a tiny amount of leftover influence might still exist, it should be so minimal that no one can misuse it.

Efficiency

Unlearning should be quick and completed within any legal time limit set by privacy laws. The process should also be limited in terms of computing resources; thus, it does not become too expensive or slow.

Utility

After the unlearning process, the model should still perform just as well on the remaining data. In other words, its overall accuracy and usefulness should not be negatively affected.

1.4 UNLEARNING FRAMEWORK

The typical steps involved in machine unlearning—a process that allows a machine learning model to forget specific pieces of data when asked—are illustrated in Figure 1.2. Generally, the workflow starts like any other ML system: the model is trained on a dataset and then used to make predictions or decisions, a process known as inference. However, when a user requests that their data be deleted, the system must go a step further. It not only removes the data from storage but also makes the model forget any influence that the data have on its learning. This is where the concept of unlearning comes in [9, 10].

Machine unlearning is essentially the process of selective forgetting. It relies on mathematical methods to reverse the learning effects of specific data points. Think of it like trying to 'undo' the learning caused by certain inputs. Each piece of data subtly adjusts the internal settings—or parameters—of the model during training. To unlearn, the system must recognize and reverse those specific changes, which is a delicate and complex task.

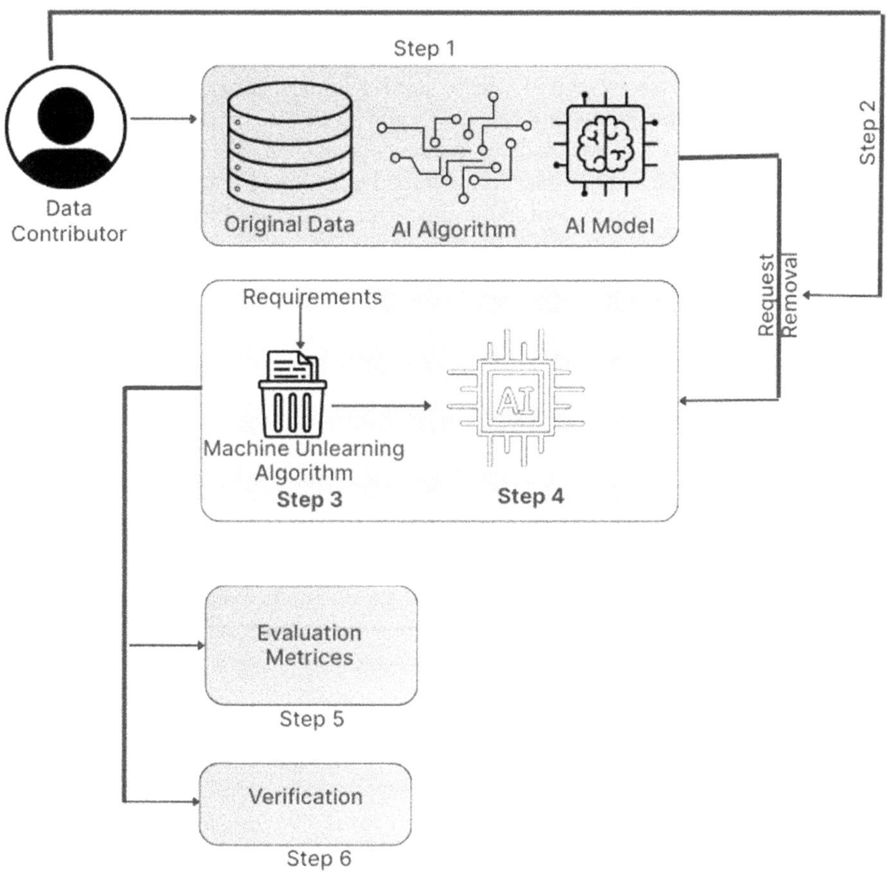

FIGURE 1.2 Machine unlearning framework.

First, the model is trained via the full dataset via a standard learning algorithm. Once a deletion request is made, the system triggers an unlearning component, which consists of an unlearning algorithm, a revised model (post-unlearning), certain performance and privacy requirements, evaluation tools, and a verification process. The goal is to eliminate the influence of specific data without damaging the model's overall performance or violating privacy.

There are several methods available to perform this unlearning. The most straightforward—but also the most expensive and time-consuming—approach is to remove the data and retrain the model from scratch. This guarantees that the data are gone, but it is not efficient, especially for large-scale systems. A more practical alternative is weight adjustment, where the model's internal settings are directly altered to cancel out the impact of the removed data. This eliminates the need for full retraining. Another method involves regularization techniques, which apply penalties during training to encourage the model to "forget" specific information. A newer and more advanced approach is called differential unlearning, which works by identifying the exact changes made to the model by specific data points and then carefully reversing just those changes.

After unlearning is completed, the new model is tested via evaluation metrics such as accuracy, the zero-retrain forgetting score, or the anamnesis index to ensure that it still performs well. However, more importantly, a privacy verification or audit is required to prove that the model no longer retains any trace of the deleted data. This audit may include techniques such as membership inference attacks (to check if the model still "remembers" that data), feature injection tests, and other "forgetting" measurements.

To support these methods and make unlearning faster and more reliable, additional tools have been developed. For example, model versioning allows the system to save snapshots of the model at different stages, making it easier to return to a previous version before the data are added. Data sanitization layers can be integrated into the training process to continuously detect and filter out data marked for deletion. Additionally, checkpoint systems, which regularly save model progress, enable quick rollbacks to earlier states without needing to be retrained from scratch.

1.5 UNLEARNING REQUESTS

Since machine learning (ML) is used in many different applications—from product recommendations to medical predictions—the way we "unlearn" data must also adapt to fit the situation. Not all unlearning requests are the same. In terms of what needs to be forgotten, there are five common types of unlearning requests, each with unique challenges and goals [11–13].

1. **Item removal:** The most straightforward and frequent type of unlearning request involves the removal of a particular data point, also known as item removal. Think of this as removing a single review from an online store's recommendation system. In many cases, users may ask for the system to forget the specific products they interact with or individual actions they perform. Similarly, in graph-based models (used in situations such as social networks), certain nodes (people) or edges (connections) might need to be

forgotten. In natural language models, this could involve forgetting specific sentences or entire documents, since individual words (or tokens) often do not carry meaningful context on their own.

2. **Feature removal:** Sometimes, the issue is not with a single item but with a group of data that shares a particular feature or attribute. For example, if a spam detection model has been tricked by thousands of emails containing the same malicious domain, removing just one email will not be enough. Instead, the model must forget everything related to that domain name. Similarly, if a job application model has been trained using biased data that consider gender or race unfairly, it needs to unlearn that entire feature across thousands of examples. In creative models such as text-to-image systems, the model may need to forget an artist's style if the copyright is violated. This type of unlearning is more complex because it targets a broader pattern within the data, not just a single piece of it.
3. **Class removal:** Class removal goes a step further by aiming to remove all knowledge associated with a particular category or group. This is common in classification problems—such as facial recognition—where each class could represent an individual. If someone opts out of such a system, the model must forget everything it learned about their face. In language models, each class might even represent a word in the vocabulary. This kind of unlearning is more difficult than removing an individual item because the data are usually distributed across the model. Simply retraining the model multiple times might be an option, but it is expensive and time consuming. Moreover, because classification models rely on learning differences between classes, completely removing one class can disrupt the balance of the whole system.
4. **Task removal:** Modern ML models often learn multiple tasks at once—such as answering questions, translating languages, and writing code. This is inspired by how the human brain works, where learning tasks in combination often help us perform better. For example, LLMs are first trained on broad, generic tasks and then fine-tuned for specific applications such as medical advice or customer support. However, sometimes a user may request that a model forget a particular task—for instance, if the task involves sensitive, client-specific information. In such cases, the model must unlearn a whole skill or function rather than just a data point. This is a complex but increasingly relevant form of unlearning, as models are used in more personalized and multifunctional ways.
5. **Stream removal:** In dynamic systems, data do not just arrive all at once—a data item flows in like a stream. The same is true for deletion requests. In stream removal, the system needs to handle a steady flow of unlearning requests over time. Many users ask that their data be deleted one after another or that an adversarial attack be discovered gradually, prompting the removal of poisonous data in phases. Sometimes these requests come independently (nonadaptive), but other times, they depend on previous changes to the model (adaptive). For example, after the first few pieces of bad data are removed, the system may better identify which data to delete

next. Managing this type of unlearning requires smart strategies to keep the model efficient and accurate even while it is constantly being updated.

1.6 DESIGN REQUIREMENTS

1. **Completeness (consistency):** One of the key qualities of a good machine unlearning method is completeness, also referred to as consistency. This means that after a model has "forgotten" certain data, its behavior should be nearly identical to that of a model that was fully retrained without that data. In simpler terms, whether the model gives a correct or incorrect answer, it should respond the same way as a freshly retrained model would. To measure how close the unlearned model is to the retrained model, researchers often compare how both models perform on a test dataset—checking what percentage of predictions match. In fact, this idea can be built directly into how we define or design unlearning by mathematically minimizing the difference between the outputs of the two models. Interestingly, the same techniques used in adversarial attacks (which test model vulnerabilities) can also help shape these consistency measurements.
2. **Timeliness:** Although retraining a model from scratch after removing some data is the most complete way to ensure unlearning, it is also time consuming and computationally expensive—especially when we do not even know exactly what needs to be forgotten. For this reason, there needs to be a balance between timeliness (how fast unlearning can happen) and completeness. Faster unlearning methods that do not require retraining might not always be perfectly complete; they can sometimes leave behind traces of the forgotten data, leading to potential privacy risks. To measure timeliness, we can compare how quickly the unlearning process works versus full retraining. Generally, when only a small portion of the data needs to be forgotten, unlearning is faster and does not affect the model much. However, if a large amount of data must be removed, retraining might be more effective, as repeatedly applying unlearning could slowly damage the model's overall accuracy.
3. **Accuracy:** Unlearning should not be such that it negatively impacts the accuracy of the model. This means that correct predictions should continue to be made, especially on new test data. Ideally, the accuracy of the unlearned model should be close to that of a retrained model. However, because retraining is expensive and often not practical for comparison, researchers instead test the unlearned model's performance on fresh data or compare it to how the model performs before any unlearning takes place. Maintaining accuracy while forgetting specific data is a difficult but essential part of building reliable unlearning systems.
4. **Lightweight:** For unlearning to work efficiently in real-world systems, the algorithm needs to be lightweight—meaning that it should not require many extra resources. Many current methods need to store model checkpoints, keep track of previous training steps, or save large amounts of temporary data. This storage and processing demand can be a serious bottleneck,

especially with large-scale models and big data. A well-designed unlearning solution should use minimal memory and processing power and avoid unnecessary overhead beyond the time and space required for unlearning itself.

5. **Provable guarantees:** Unlike retraining, which yields near-perfect results, most unlearning methods rely on approximations. This means that they try to become as close as possible to the retrained model without actually performing full retraining. Because of this, it is important that these methods offer provable guarantees—basically, mathematical assurances that unlearning has been performed properly within certain bounds. Many techniques now include such guarantees by showing that if two models have similar internal parameters, they should perform similarly on tasks. These types of safeguards make unlearning more trustworthy.
6. **Model-agnostic:** Ideally, an unlearning method should be model-agnostic—it should work across different types of machine learning models (such as neural networks, decision trees, etc.) and training algorithms. This flexibility makes it easier to apply unlearning in different applications without the need to redesign the method every time. However, this is easier said than done. Since different models learn in different ways, creating one unlearning framework that fits all can be very challenging.
7. **Verifiability:** Last, a good unlearning system should give users confidence that their data have truly been forgotten. This means that the model should include some kind of verification mechanism—something users can use to check that the unlearning was successful. One way researchers test this is by inserting "backdoor" data into the training set and checking whether it still appears in the unlearned model. If it's gone, that's a sign the unlearning worked. However, this type of testing is not always practical or safe. It might introduce errors (false positives) or new risks into the system. Therefore, building nonintrusive but effective ways for users to verify unlearning is still an open challenge.

1.7 MACHINE UNLEARNING APPLICATIONS

In addition to the inherent demands of machine unlearning, which has drawn much research attention, many researchers have reported that machine unlearning can be applied in many other scenarios to solve related problems.

1.7.1 Unlearning in Recommender Systems

Recommender systems are a central part of modern machine learning and are used everywhere, from online shopping platforms to streaming services and social media. Their job is to help users discover content they are likely to enjoy—such as suggesting a new movie to watch, a product to buy, or an article to read. They help users navigate overwhelming amounts of information by offering personalized suggestions, and this personalization is made possible through a method called collaborative filtering. Collaborative filtering analyzes a user's past behavior—like what they have clicked on, viewed, rated, or purchased—and finds patterns to predict what they might want next [13–15].

However, as these systems learn from historical user data, they often store and remember specific user interactions in their models. This raises concerns about user privacy. There may be situations where a user wants to have their data completely removed—not only from the database but also from the model itself. Such requests could be due to privacy laws such as the GDPR or personal preferences. In other cases, unlearning is requested for utility reasons, such as removing inaccurate or irrelevant data that could skew the model's recommendations. This makes machine unlearning a critical need for recommender systems [16].

A straightforward but costly way to forget a user's data is to retrain the entire recommendation model from scratch, excluding that user's data. However, for large-scale systems that handle millions of users and items, this method is computationally expensive and impractical. Therefore, more efficient unlearning approaches have emerged. Unlike typical machine learning tasks such as image or text classification, recommender systems address interaction data—user-item relationships that are interconnected and rich in collaborative signals. This makes unlearning more complicated. To address these challenges, researchers have proposed LASER, a model-agnostic unlearning framework designed specifically for recommendation systems [17]. LASER breaks the dataset into smaller parts (or shards) and trains the model sequentially on each part. This approach helps retain collaborative signals even while enabling the efficient unlearning of specific users. It balances both performance and privacy and performs better than traditional models do in terms of maintaining recommendation quality. Another method [18] takes a different route by aiming to randomize the model's predictions for the sequences or data it needs to forget. Instead of just erasing data, this method gradually changes the model's understanding of that data so that it becomes less confident in its original assumption. The use of a dynamic process that modifies incorrect labels during training prevents the model from learning the wrong things while also pushing it to forget the original labels.

As privacy becomes a greater concern, attribute unlearning has emerged as a powerful tool to prevent privacy breaches, such as attribute inference attacks, where a person can guess sensitive user information (such as gender or age) on the basis of the model's behavior [19]. In response, researchers have designed pluggable attribute unlearning frameworks, which add a special "erasure" module to the recommender system. This module can remove the impact of certain private attributes, and if a user later changes their mind, the module can even reverse the unlearning. In short, as recommender systems become more powerful and widespread, developing efficient, flexible, and privacy-respecting unlearning methods becomes just as important as improving their predictive accuracy.

1.7.2 Unlearning Federated Learning

Federated learning (FL) has become increasingly important in the field of machine learning, especially in areas where data privacy is a major concern—such as healthcare. In a typical FL setup, instead of collecting all the sensitive data (such as patient records) in a central place, as noted earlier, the data stay on the devices where they are generated—such as hospital servers or personal computers. These devices, known as clients, train the machine learning model locally via private data. Afterward, only the updated model parameters (not the raw data) are sent to a central server, which combines updates from all the clients to construct a better global model. In this way, personal data never leave the client's device, making the process more privacy friendly [20–22]. However, if someone later wants their data removed from the system (for privacy or legal reasons), things become tricky. The most straightforward solution is to delete the data on the client and retrain the entire federated model from scratch. However, this approach is extremely time consuming and computationally expensive, especially when many clients are involved.

To address this, researchers have started working on federated unlearning (FUL), a method to efficiently "forget" a client's contribution without having to retrain the entire model. This is even more challenging in the FL setting because the data are distributed across clients and are not centrally available [23]. One promising solution involves a two-step process. First, the client that wants its data to be erased runs a local unlearning procedure to undo its contribution. This locally unlearned model is then sent back to the server, which performs just a few more communication rounds with the remaining clients to update the global model. This strategy avoids the need for access to the entire training dataset or a record of all past updates [24].

Despite these advances, federated unlearning is still an evolving area with open challenges. For example, many current methods rely heavily on retraining-based calibration, which not only is inefficient but also may introduce new privacy risks. Additionally, most of today's efficient unlearning techniques work well only for simpler models (such as those used in convex optimization problems) and struggle with complex models such as deep neural networks. To address these problems, a new approach called FedRecovery was introduced by researchers [20]. This method applies differential privacy—a technique that adds controlled randomness to protect individual data. FedRecovery works by removing the influence of a client from the global model via a calculated adjustment of the gradients (i.e., how much each client's data changed the model). It also adds Gaussian noise to ensure that the updated model is statistically indistinguishable from one that was retrained without the erased client's data. This makes the process both efficient and privacy preserving, pushing the field of federated unlearning forward.

1.7.3 Unlearning in Graph Embedding

In most machine unlearning research thus far, the data are typically assumed to be independent—meaning that each piece of data is treated separately from the rest. However, in many real-world applications, data are relational rather than isolated. This is where graphs come into play. Graphs are powerful tools that help represent interconnected systems. For example, in a social network, each person can be seen as a node, and their friendships form edges. Graphs are also used in biology (such as protein interactions), transport systems, and many other fields. They offer a compact and flexible way to understand complex relationships and make better decisions or predictions [25]. Understanding the structure of these graphs is key to solving problems in such domains. However, in terms of machine unlearning in graph-based models, the situation becomes much more complicated. One major challenge is that the data are interconnected—removing one piece can affect many others. Unlike in regular datasets, the graph cannot be split easily because the connections between nodes matter. Additionally, unlearning requests in graph data can refer to either nodes (entities) or edges (relationships), both of which may affect the model differently. Furthermore, graph structures are often uneven, meaning that some parts are densely connected, whereas others are sparse. This imbalance can make it difficult to retrain the model fairly efficiently after unlearning [26].

To handle these complexities, we need advanced algorithms that can carefully "forget" specific parts of a graph without breaking its overall structure or usefulness. For example, one of the first known methods for nonlinear graph unlearning uses a technique called graph spectral transforms and offers a theoretical look at how complex this process truly is [27]. In the specific case of knowledge graphs—which represent entities and the relationships between them in a structured form—knowledge graph embedding methods are used to translate this structure into mathematical vectors that computers can easily work with. These embeddings are useful in tasks such as answering questions or predicting missing links in the graph. A newer approach called metaEU (meta-learning-based embedding unlearning) [28] makes it possible to unlearn knowledge from these embeddings in a smarter way. Instead of starting every time a user wants their data removed, MetaEU learns patterns across different unlearning tasks, making the process faster and more generalizable.

1.7.4 Unlearning in Lifelong Learning

Machine unlearning is not always a drawback; in some cases, it can actually help improve the accuracy and reliability of a machine learning model. One common issue in deep learning is catastrophic forgetting, where a model "forgets" what it previously learned when it was trained on new tasks. This is a serious problem in scenarios where models are expected to handle multiple or evolving tasks over time. A simple but flawed solution would be to retrain the model using all the previous data, but this approach is highly inefficient—it consumes many computational resources and time. Even worse, there is no guarantee that the model will relearn everything correctly or that forgetting will not happen again. To address this, researchers such as Du et al. [29] proposed an interesting approach that uses machine unlearning as a way to guard against catastrophic forgetting. Instead of retraining from scratch, their method involves identifying and removing harmful or misleading data points (such as false positives or false negatives), which may contribute to model confusion. After unlearning these problematic samples, the model is updated such that its past performance is preserved and further degradation is prevented. In this context, unlearning becomes a positive tool—not just for privacy or regulation—but also as a proactive way to maintain and even enhance a model's accuracy over time.

1.7.5 Unlearning in Large Language Models

LLMs, such as ChatGPT and GPT-4, have shown remarkable capabilities across a wide range of tasks, from writing and translation to coding and creative content generation. This success is largely due to their training on massive amounts of text data, which enables them to learn patterns and generalize well. However, as these models grow more powerful, concerns around data privacy, ethics, and regulatory compliance have also increased. Regulations such as the GDPR in Europe and the CCPA in the United States require individuals to have the right to request the deletion of their personal data. In the context of LLMs, this creates a significant challenge—because these models can inadvertently memorize and reproduce sensitive, outdated, or copyrighted information that was present in their training data. To address this, machine unlearning techniques are being explored for LLMs. These methods aim to selectively remove the influence of specific data points from a trained model without retraining it entirely from scratch. This is particularly important when trying to erase inaccurate, confidential, or obsolete information. However, applying unlearning to LLMs is especially difficult because of their scale and complexity [30–32]. One major obstacle is that, for privacy or copyright reasons, the original data may no longer be accessible when an unlearning request is made. Without access to that data, it is difficult to ensure that the model "forgets" it properly without compromising overall performance. Thus, current research is focused on developing efficient, targeted unlearning approaches that can preserve the model's usefulness while respecting privacy and legal obligations.

REFERENCES

1. Bourtoule, L., Chandrasekaran, V., Choquette-Choo, C. A., Jia, H., Travers, A., Zhang, B., . . . & Papernot, N. (2021, May). Machine unlearning. In 2021 IEEE symposium on security and privacy (SP) (pp. 141–159). IEEE.
2. Nguyen, T. T., Huynh, T. T., Ren, Z., Nguyen, P. L., Liew, A. W. C., Yin, H., & Nguyen, Q. V. H. (2022). A survey of machine unlearning. arXiv preprint arXiv:2209.02299.
3. Tarun, A. K., Chundawat, V. S., Mandal, M., & Kankanhalli, M. (2023). Fast yet effective machine unlearning. IEEE Transactions on Neural Networks and Learning Systems, 35(9), 13046–13055.
4. Cao, Y., & Yang, J. (2015, May). Toward making systems forget with machine unlearning. In 2015 IEEE symposium on security and privacy (pp. 463–480). IEEE.
5. Zhang, H., Nakamura, T., Isohara, T., & Sakurai, K. (2023). A review on machine unlearning. SN Computer Science, 4(4), 337.
6. Xu, J., Wu, Z., Wang, C., & Jia, X. (2024). Machine unlearning: Solutions and challenges. IEEE Transactions on Emerging Topics in Computational Intelligence, 8(3), 2150–2168.
7. Ali, Z., Muhammad, A., Adnan, R., Alkhalifah, T., & Aslam, S. (2025). Evaluating machine unlearning: Applications, approaches, and accuracy. Engineering Reports, 7(1), e13081.
8. Shaik, T., Tao, X., Xie, H., Li, L., Zhu, X., & Li, Q. (2024). Exploring the landscape of machine unlearning: A comprehensive survey and taxonomy. IEEE Transactions on Neural Networks and Learning Systems, 36(7), 11676–11696. https://doi.org/10.1109/TNNLS.2024.3486109
9. Nguyen, T. T., Huynh, T. T., Ren, Z., Nguyen, P. L., Liew, A. W. C., Yin, H., & Nguyen, Q. V. H. (2022). A survey of machine unlearning. arXiv preprint arXiv:2209.02299.
10. Li, N., Zhou, C., Gao, Y., Chen, H., Zhang, Z., Kuang, B., & Fu, A. (2025). Machine unlearning: Taxonomy, metrics, applications, challenges, and prospects. IEEE Transactions on Neural Networks and Learning Systems, 36(8), 13709–13729. https://doi.org/10.1109/TNNLS.2025.3530988

11. Liu, Z., Ye, H., Chen, C., Zheng, Y., & Lam, K. Y. (2025). Threats, attacks, and defenses in machine unlearning: A survey. IEEE Open Journal of the Computer Society, 6, 413–425. https://doi.org/10.1109/OJCS.2025.3543483
12. Sekhari, A., Acharya, J., Kamath, G., & Suresh, A. T. (2021). Remember what you want to forget: Algorithms for machine unlearning. Advances in Neural Information Processing Systems, 34, 18075–18086.
13. Li, C., Jiang, H., Chen, J., Zhao, Y., Fu, S., Jing, F., & Guo, Y. (2025). An overview of machine unlearning. High-Confidence Computing, 5(2), 100254.
14. Chen, C., Zhang, Y., Li, Y., Wang, J., Qi, L., Xu, X., . . . & Yin, J. (2024). Posttraining attribute unlearning in recommender systems. ACM Transactions on Information Systems, 43(1), 1–28.
15. Sachdeva, B., Rathee, H., Sristi, Sharma, A., & Wydmański, W. (2024, February). Machine unlearning for recommendation systems: An insight. In International conference on innovative computing and communication (pp. 415–430). Singapore: Springer Nature Singapore.
16. Chen, C., Sun, F., Zhang, M., & Ding, B. (2022, April). Recommendation unlearning. In Proceedings of the ACM web conference 2022 (pp. 2768–2777).
17. Li, Y., Chen, C., Zheng, X., Liu, J., & Wang, J. (2024). Making recommender systems forget: Learning and unlearning for erasable recommendation. Knowledge-Based Systems, 283, 111124.
18. Ye, S., & Lu, J. (2023, November). Sequence unlearning for sequential recommender systems. In Australasian joint conference on artificial intelligence (pp. 403–415). Singapore: Springer Nature Singapore.
19. Feng, X., Li, Y., Yu, F., Zhang, L., Chen, C., & Zheng, X. (2025, April). Plug and play: Enabling pluggable attribute unlearning in recommender systems. In Proceedings of the ACM on web conference 2025 (pp. 2689–2699).
20. Zhang, L., Zhu, T., Zhang, H., Xiong, P., & Zhou, W. (2023). Fedrecovery: Differentially private machine unlearning for federated learning frameworks. IEEE Transactions on Information Forensics and Security, 18, 4732–4746.
21. Ding, N., Sun, Z., Wei, E., & Berry, R. (2023, October). Incentive mechanism design for federated learning and unlearning. In Proceedings of the Twenty-fourth international symposium on theory, algorithmic foundations, and protocol design for mobile networks and mobile computing (pp. 11–20).
22. Ameen, M., Khan, R. U., Wang, P., Batool, S., & Alajmi, M. (2024). Addressing unreliable local models in federated learning through unlearning. Neural Networks, 180, 106688.
23. Halimi, A., Kadhe, S., Rawat, A., & Baracaldo, N. (2022). Federated unlearning: How to efficiently erase a client in FL? arXiv preprint arXiv:2207.05521.
24. Liu, Z., Jiang, Y., Shen, J., Peng, M., Lam, K. Y., Yuan, X., & Liu, X. (2024). A survey on federated unlearning: Challenges, methods, and future directions. ACM Computing Surveys, 57(1), 1–38.
25. Said, A., Zhao, Y., Derr, T., Shabbir, M., Abbas, W., & Koutsoukos, X. (2023). A survey of graph unlearning. arXiv preprint arXiv:2310.02164.
26. Said, A., Zhao, Y., Derr, T., Shabbir, M., Abbas, W., & Koutsoukos, X. (2023). A survey of graph unlearning. arXiv preprint arXiv:2310.02164.
27. Pan, C., Chien, E., & Milenkovic, O. (2023, April). Unlearning graph classifiers with limited data resources. In Proceedings of the ACM web conference 2023 (pp. 716–726).
28. Xu, N., Li, Q., Li, Z., Wang, X., Liu, B., Mpofu, J. B., . . . & Li, X. (2025). Learn to unlearn: Meta-learning-based knowledge graph embedding unlearning. Knowledge and Information Systems, 1–22.

29. Du, M., Chen, Z., Liu, C., Oak, R., & Song, D. (2019, November). Lifelong anomaly detection through unlearning. In Proceedings of the 2019 ACM SIGSAC conference on computer and communications security (pp. 1283–1297).
30. Liu, S., Yao, Y., Jia, J., Casper, S., Baracaldo, N., Hase, P., . . . & Liu, Y. (2025). Rethinking machine unlearning for large language models. Nature Machine Intelligence, 1–14.
31. Yao, Y., Xu, X., & Liu, Y. (2024). Large language model unlearning. Advances in Neural Information Processing Systems, 37, 105425–105475.
32. Yuan, X., Pang, T., Du, C., Chen, K., Zhang, W., & Lin, M. (2024). A closer look at machine unlearning for large language models. arXiv preprint arXiv:2410.08109.

2 Technological Approaches to Unlearning

2.1 TECHNOLOGICAL APPROACHES TO UNLEARNING

The privacy of data and user control has gained new significance with the more widespread implementation of machine learning (ML) systems in everyday technologies, including search engines and recommendation systems, as well as in medical diagnosis and predictive policing. The issue of whether and by what means data already viewed can be forgotten by systems has become increasingly important because data have become among the core resources in the automated decision-making process. It is a morally as well as a legally problematic issue. The right to be forgotten or the right to have the data removed is defined in legislation such as the California Consumer Privacy Act (CCPA) and the General Data Protection Regulation (GDPR). Removing a row in a database is easy, but it is much more difficult to remove the effect of that information on the performance of a machine learning model that has already been trained on it. In this regard, machine unlearning, a new field of AI, has come into play. It aims at effectively and efficiently removing the effect of specific data in models with minimum disturbance. Technological approaches to unlearning are aimed at achieving a balance between scalability and compliance, privacy and utility, and forgetting and performance. These approaches can be grouped into four broad categories: architecture-aware strategies, certified unlearning, approximate unlearning, and retraining-based approaches. They all possess their own areas of appropriateness, practice constraints, and trade-offs (see Figure 2.1).

The retraining paradigm [1, 2] is the basis of technological unlearning. The assumption behind this approach is that the only sure way to forget data is to destroy the existing model and retrain it with only permitted data. In theory, this would be intuitively perceived as forgetting: a fresh start without exposure to the data under consideration. Retraining is easy, predictive, and very stringent in terms of compliance with requirements. It removes any potential impact that the deleted data could have had, provided that the auxiliary artifacts such as optimizer states or logs are also deleted. However, the scalability of retraining is a problem. The deep neural networks trained on high-dimensional data are computationally costly to reconstruct. Even tasks involving image classification [3] of moderate size may require hours or days to retrain. Retraining is practically infeasible in dynamic data environments, where the data of the user are actively updated or revoked [3]. Despite these limitations, retraining remains the gold standard in research on empirical unlearning. Any new method that purports to forget must, in the ideal scenario, have an equal amount

 DOI: 10.1201/9781003771470-2

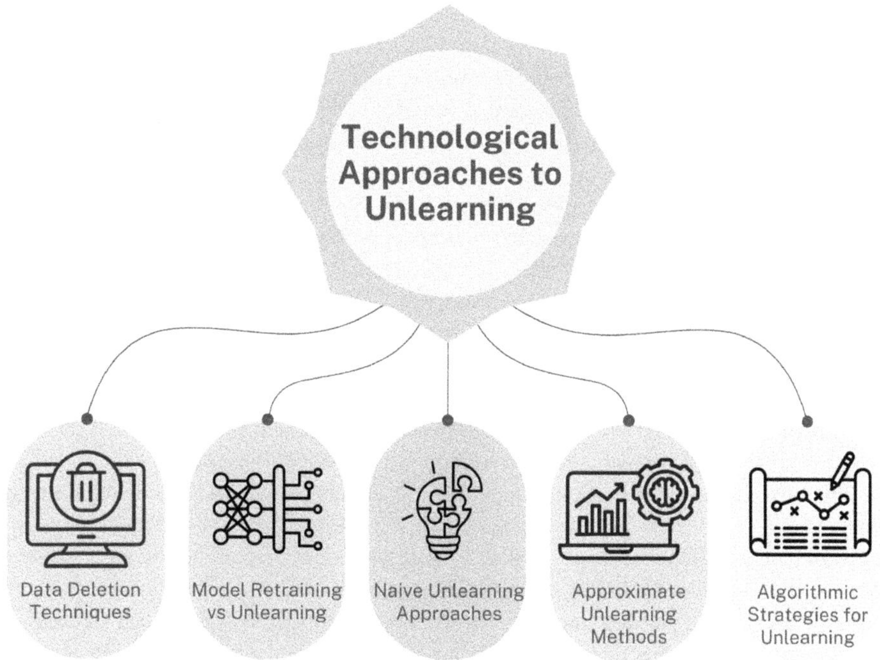

FIGURE 2.1 Technological approaches to unlearning.

of performance degradation on the deleted data and an equal amount of model accuracy on the retained data.

To eliminate the drawbacks of complete retraining [4–6], scientists have suggested approximate unlearning techniques to imitate the impact of eliminating data at a steeply diminished computational cost. These include approaches that are based on influence that quantify and reverse the effects of data points on model parameters by methods in robust statistics. Influence functions [7], originally presented in classical statistics, were altered by Koh et al. to apply them to machine learning. These roles allow a model to reverse-learn its learned representations by estimating the effect of removing a training point on the loss on a test input. Although it has this potential, the approach is limited by assumptions of convexity and smooth loss surfaces, which are not often satisfied by modern deep learning models. Moreover, calculating the second-order derivatives and their inverses on a large scale is expensive. Nonetheless, the concept of influence-based unlearning provides a convenient approach to data influence as a graded flow process, as opposed to a fixed artifact, which can be reverted. Gradient correction techniques are another field of approximate unlearning that extends past influence functions. The methods reverse the path of the model by subtracting the gradients associated with the removed data in the parameter space. These techniques are challenging when the training of models [8, 9] is not locally linearly separable or when the removed data create nonlinear shifts in the parameter space, although they are more computationally economical than influence functions are. These models often require stored gradient information during training, and this may be problematic in terms of storage and privacy Nevertheless, because gradient correction [10] can achieve accelerated unlearning with a loss that is limited in accuracy, it remains a research issue. Selective retraining is also a good approximation method that has gained popularity, especially in architectures where certain layers are more sensitive to training data than others are. In convolutional neural networks, an example is that the higher layers are learned to represent a specific class, whereas the lower layers are learned to be general purpose such as edges or textures. Data-specific influence can be removed by retraining only specific layers or modules, without necessarily rebuilding the model at all. This has been explored in both the context of transfer learning and modular deep learning, where performance retention and forgetting can be achieved by updating certain parts of the model and freezing others. This approach, however, is dependent on architecture design and assumes that they can easily isolate the influence of data, which is difficult in networks that have numerous connections.

The introduction of certified unlearning—a method in which the formal claim is made that a model has forgotten particular information—is a more recent development in technological unlearning. These methods aim at narrowing the gap between theory and practice. Golatkar et al. (2020) proposed [6] the concept of forgetting events whereby the performance on erased data of a model is deliberately decreased without negatively affecting the performance on retained data. It aims to modify the internal representations such that it proves the loss of information and not just to lower the accuracy of forgotten samples. Statistical and probabilistic certification [11, 12] methods are also certified unlearning methods and strive to find an approximation of how similar models are when trained on the Pre-removal data versus when the data are removed. Unlearning is considered successful when the two models do not differ statistically. The particular strategies are in conformity with the requirements of explainability, with explainability tools that demonstrate the effect of deletion. The other application of certified unlearning is information theory. These techniques add the concept of unlearning as mutual information minimization/reduction of entropy, in which the task is to minimize information learned by a model on a point of data removed. Such guarantees tend to be institutionalized as a distinction of privacy methods. Privacy budget-aware models can be trained to limit the size of the data-specific influence of a model following removal. Privacy-preserving training offers a system in which one can easily quantify forgetting but not unlearning. In their certified removal model, Gupta et al. speculated [13] on this notion by applying formal proofs to the idea that models that have been trained on a given algorithm are expected not to disclose a deleted user. These promises are not certain, but they are likely to lead to law abidance.

Changes in architecture are contributing to facilitating unlearning in the realm of practical system design. Division of data into distinct groups and subsequent training in isolation is known as partitioned learning, in which the model can be retrained any time in the case of deletion. It is also comparable to the sharded, isolated, and sliced aggregated (SISA) training framework suggested by Bourtoule et al., where datasets [1] are distributed on shards and slices and isolated such that the effects of a single data point can be limited to a single slice. The retraining of the respective slices of a data point is needed when it is not needed, and the rebuilt model may be recreated through the process of aggregation. SISA [14–16] is also efficient, and in contrast to the other models, it does not affect model accuracy in favor of model retrainability, nor does it have to be applied where deletions are frequent and perfection is not of the highest priority. Knowledge distillation refers to a new model (student) trained to yield the same result as the original model (the teacher) but with no access to the information that should not be considered. This facilitates the creation of a new model that mimics the actions of the teacher and ends up being independent of the information that has just been deleted. Model pruning, quantization, or compression can be used to make the unlearning process even more efficient. Despite the roughness of distillation [17] as a tool, which cannot guarantee the complete removal of influence, it is a helpful construct for constructing forgetful models without having to retrain the original.

Unlearning involving federated learning is decentralized unlearning. Information in the federation is saved on local computers, and only updates are shared with a centralized server. This provides a default way of deletion at the user level, as local models could be reset or retrained individually. Such tools as FedEraser [12] are designed to remove the contributions of a user, just by subtracting them in the global model, by changing the parameters. The greatest problem is ensuring that these subtractions are mathematically correct and that they do not bias global convergence. Model staleness, data correlation, and aggregation are some problems with federated unlearning and make the deletion process more difficult. Nonetheless, federated learning is closely related to the goals of user autonomy and local control; thus, it is a good direction for future research in unlearning. As machine unlearning becomes an area of study, human engagement in engineering functionality becomes more significant. The technologies that allow complete forgetting at the cost of inefficiency may not be applicable in real life, and methods that aim at speed may not be able to fulfill legal and ethical demands. A compromise can be so-called hybrid solutions, for example, approximate approaches to day-to-day deletion and certified retraining of high-risk data. Additionally, explainability and uncertainty quantification tools may be more important for helping auditors, developers, and users acquire knowledge about the limits and guarantees of unlearning mechanisms. As the models continue to grow increasingly larger and closer to human activity, selective forgetting stops being a feature that is created when the designers of the AI mean well but is also created by it.

2.2 UNLEARNING ALGORITHM STRATEGIES

Since the demand for responsible and regulation-aware machine learning systems has increased, the challenge introduced by the need to forget certain training data without negatively affecting the overall utility of a model has become one of the key technical issues. The traditional machine learning algorithms [18–20] are accumulative; the algorithm is optimized to learn all of the available data and remember generalized patterns and be more effective as it is trained on more data. However, this continued memorization becomes troublesome in the environment where users request that their data be erased for privacy reasons, fairness reasons, or legal reasons. A proactive way out of this dilemma is provided by algorithmic approaches to unlearning. Instead of using only system-level resets or haphazard retraining, these methods incorporate unlearning logic in the training pipeline itself. They pay attention to algorithmic methods, which allow them to systematically eliminate or cancel the impact of specific data points on model predictions or parameters. It is aimed not only at eliminating data but also at undoing its impact in a way that is preferably verifiable and computationally inexpensive. The concept of data influence modeling [21] is at the core of algorithmic unlearning. It defines the contribution of one piece of data or a collection of data to the final model. These classical machine learning models, such as linear regression and support vector machines, have tractable approximations of this influence because they are convex and often form closed-form models. As an illustration, in stochastic gradient descent (SGD) applied to a convex problem, the removal of a data point can be estimated by reverting the gradient update of the data point. Theoretically, when a model is trained on a known sequence of updates, it is possible to reverse the effects of a specific sample by taking the gradient step [10] of that sample and reversing it. This reverse gradient method, however, assumes a constant optimizer state, learning rate, and data sequence, all of which are not frequently maintained in real-world use, at least when deep learning models are used. In addition, with nonconvex settings, a model path in parameter space is very sensitive to the sequence order of updates; that is, negating a gradient does not always reverse the effect of the data. Such constraints have led to the development of more algorithm designs that incorporate forgetting steps in a more structured manner within training algorithms. An example of such an algorithm is updating efficient training algorithms that are designed to support post hoc editing of the training record. The training algorithm is not used sequentially in its training steps; rather, it is more modular in that it uses SGD in a sequential manner. As an example, the SISA training strategy [1] breaks the training data into various shards and slices. Independent training of each slice of the model and deletion is achieved by retraining only that slice of the model that represents the data to be forgotten. Although this is sometimes referred to as system-level optimization, it is also an indication of an evolution of training algorithm design that places more emphasis on isolation of influence. A localized influence pattern [22] is effectively imposed by the SISA slicing mechanism, which facilitates the controlled propagation of deletion. It is scalable and approximate unlearning because the algorithm does not require retraining the whole model; it only attempts to unlearn a particular data point in a module during the training phase.

The other interesting algorithmic paradigm is the influence of function-based training modification. The concept of influence functions, which is a version of classical robust statistics adjusted to machine learning using Koh and Liang (2017), is used to estimate the changes in the forecasts of a model when a specific data point is added or removed. During training, they are used to track samples whose influence on model behavior is disproportionately large and possibly to reoptimize paths as well. Recent research has extended this with more recent work, further elaborating some models that dynamically tune their sensitivity to training data according to desired unlearning [23] guarantees. By doing so, performance metrics are not the only criteria by which the training algorithm is guided: also by removability constraints. They can be trained in an explicit way, for example, by reducing some loss which penalizes the influence of individual data points, thus making the model more forgetful by design. Another progressively important and more influential category of algorithms is certifiability in training. In this model, the algorithm not only learns by data but also renders a certificate that is usually probabilistic or statistical and attests to the extent to which any given sample affects the final model. One of them is the idea of certified removal provided by Gupta et al., where the training algorithm [13] is trained to provide post hoc reasoning stating that a specific data sample does not substantially influence the model output once it has been deleted. This will necessitate special loss formulations [24] and training mechanisms that strike a balance between accuracy and removability in the future. Such algorithms can improve the ability to unlearn at the expense of a viable compromise with training efficiency or predictive accuracy (a training procedure that is not just about learning well but learning reversibly).

The other potentially useful family of algorithms is that based on the principle of knowledge modularity. The objective of these algorithms is to encode knowledge of various portions of the data space into discontinuous portions of the model. As an example, mixed-of-experts models or neural networks with attention bottlenecks can be designed so that one type of information is specialized in one set of neurons or heads. The models can selectively prune or reweight the affected parts of a model without disrupting the other parts when the data need to be deleted. Although this method is more typical of NLP [25] and vision transformers, it is indicative of a broader trend of building architectures where fine-grained control of the knowledge learned can be easily achieved, allowing unlearning to occur more easily. The algorithmic unlearning strategies acquire special shapes in federated learning settings. In this case, training is decentralized, and every user contributes to the global model through local updates. Such algorithms as FedEraser modify the federated averaging process to enable user-level unlearning. In particular, they approximate and deduce the historical contribution of updates of a user to the central model after which retraining is selectively performed where necessary.

The problem is that it is computationally difficult to model and invert update aggregation correctly, particularly in asynchronous or only partially available client models. To overcome this limitation, current research has suggested federated learning algorithms that record user contributions in a decomposable manner, thus making it easy to remove and reaggregate them. These methods demonstrate that algorithmic unlearning is applicable at the model level and can be implemented in a model of communication and aggregation in distributed systems. Finally, the most prospective category of algorithmic strategies involves meta-learning and continual learning schemes designed to unlearn. These algorithms are designed to train models in a way that is intrinsically flexible in that they can easily add or remove information without significant retraining. Specifically, meta-learning algorithms enable the model to learn how to learn; that is, they can be trained to learn on new tasks or unlearn old ones by updating with only a few examples of new tasks. A fine-tuning of the meta-objective allows one to condition the model to do so to show graceful forgetting. This approach has the potential to transform the concept of unlearning, as it would concern the design of forgettable models rather than deletion by post hoc methods. Although in the nascent phases of development, these types of algorithmic innovations are indicative of a paradigm shift in how training processes can develop under the strains of contemporary data governance requirements. Altogether, unlearning algorithmic methods extend much further than optimization of the loss functions or gradient reversal. They reflect a re-engineering of the very learning process, in which reversibility, modularity, and traceability have become first-class issues alongside accuracy and efficiency. With the legal requirements and societal demands still repeating the importance of responsible AI, we are likely to see that in the future, training algorithms will not simply aim at learning [26] efficiently but also forget. The creation of such algorithms involves a profound combination of the concepts of optimization, statistics, machine learning theory, and information privacy. Devising models that can forget is difficult; but forgetting becomes a smooth, auditable, and scalable process, one that respects the dignity of the data subjects as well as maintaining the integrity of machine intelligence.

2.3 DATA DELETION TECHNIQUES

The deletion of data has been considered an initial practice in the field of data governance, especially concerning privacy-saving systems and legal adherence. Conventional methods of data deletion are often categorized into three methods: logical deletion, physical deletion, and secure deletion. Logical deletion is used to indicate records that are deleted in databases but without any physical deletion of records in databases, enabling logical deletion records to be recovered or audited. Physical deletion is the other method, where data are lost permanently by destroying the area where they exist on the disk, but the data may still be left behind unless they are overwritten. Secure deletion methods can avoid this issue by overwriting the storage sites with random bits several times to make them irrecoverable, typically to requirements such as DoD 5220.22-M [27] or NIST SP 800–88 [28]. Tools such as shred, SRM (secure remove) or full-disk encryption facilities can be used at the infrastructure [29] level to securely erase sensitive information out of file systems or storage devices. Although they are effective at the storage layer, they are only used with static datasets and do not provide any control over the impact the deleted data have had on downstream processes, such as analytics, forecasting, or machine learning model behavior. This has become especially severe in the setting of AI-based systems, where once data are fed, the system becomes miscalculated with model weights and decision-making logic in that the information is now irreversibly embedded in ways such that it cannot be removed by simply deleting the data in the database. The introduction of the machine unlearning paradigm is a direct answer to this gap since it seeks to eliminate the influence of already observed data on already trained models. In contrast to classical deletion, which sees data as passive and isolated, machine unlearning takes into account the integrated and dynamic characteristics of learning systems. It suggests algorithmic, statistical, and system-level solutions to forget the contribution of the data without having to retrain [1, 3] the entire model, which is computationally viable, thus providing an alternative way of ensuring that the obligations to the deletion of data are fulfilled. Examples of these unlearning techniques [16] are precise techniques, such as retraining on new data;

imprecise techniques, such as reversing influence functions or gradient negation; and certified unlearning, which provides demonstrable proof of data deletion. Machine unlearning is particularly important in the times of federated learning and federated AI systems, when the data are decentralized and deletion requests should be processed effectively with no access to centralized datasets. Furthermore, with legal frameworks such as the GDPR, Central Consumer Protection Authority (CCPA), and Digital Personal Data Protection Act in India focusing on the right to be forgotten of an individual, the concept of machine unlearning is becoming regarded as not only a technical advancement but also an essential aspect of ethical and legal AI. The implementation of unlearning into data pipelines, model training procedures, and system structures ensures that deletion is no longer considered a final operation performed only on raw data but rather a continuous feature that goes throughout the lifetime of a model. An emergence of machine unlearning, then, as a successor to classical approaches to deletion is a significant transformation in how we think about the phenomenon of data deletion in contemporary intelligent systems, a shift toward deletion being dynamic rather than purely erasive.

2.4 MODEL RETRAINING VERSUS UNLEARNING

Model retraining is a leading technique in the rapidly expanding field of machine unlearning, as it satisfies the urgent requirement to cleanse the effects of certain data points in a trained machine learning model without necessarily rebuilding the whole model afresh. Model retraining and machine unlearning, two concepts that have surfaced in the constantly changing environment of AI and machine learning, have become vital parts of data-driven systems management. Model retraining is a concept that signifies the act of refining an existing machine learning model with new information to achieve better performance, fit the new environment, or rectify biases. Such an iterative process is necessary to ensure the relevance and accuracy of the predictive models, especially in dynamic settings such as finance, healthcare, and e-commerce. On the other hand, machine unlearning helps eliminate some data points from the machine model training set such that the machine forgets some information without having to retrain the machine. This feature is becoming crucial in situations where privacy of data and adherence to the law matter. Researchers and practitioners must understand the differences between retraining models and machine unlearning since it impacts how machine learning [30] is designed and deployed and how it is applied ethically. In [30], the authors examine the underlying principles, methods, and consequences of both solutions and provide an overview of their positions in the lifecycle of machine learning models. The discussion of model retraining and machine unlearning involves tension between model stability and data privacy. The traditional method is model retraining, whereby the optimization and continuous improvement of machine learning models are performed by utilizing new data. This is important for maintaining accurate and effective models as time progresses, especially in areas where real-time decision-making is highly essential, such as in finance and healthcare. Through frequent model updates, organizations can use the most recent information to improve their predictive potential and sustain their competitive edges. Conversely, although machine unlearning does provide a system to detrain certain data points in a model, critical questions arise with regard to the integrity and strength of the model as a whole. The need to forget some information may create instability and unpredictability in the work of the model, especially when it is not implemented attentively. Furthermore, the emphasis on data privacy and compliance, which is necessary, must not conceal the significance of having a stable and high-performing model. The issues of machine unlearning implementation could complicate the development of the model and can create new risks that might compromise the credibility of AI systems. Therefore, even though both methods are essential, the role of model retraining as a strategy for guaranteeing the continuity of accuracy and reliability cannot be underemphasized in the broader discourse on machine learning practices. Machine unlearning [19] is a relatively new field of machine learning that aims to create effective algorithms to help a model forget certain data points. In contrast to classic retraining of the model, which involves rebuilding the model afresh or at a checkpoint, machine unlearning deliberately erases the effects of specific sets of data on a trained model. This is gaining relevance, as there is increasing concern about the privacy of data and laws such as the right to forget. To perform unlearning, the model should eliminate or counter the learned features that match the desired data subset. Scholars have come up with different methods. For example, Cao et al. proposed [24] an unlearning algorithm in the statistical query learning paradigm, where the model is not able to access single samples but is updated effectively by a small number of summations. This approach indicates that retraining can achieve much less data and time. Other methods include partial retraining, whereby the data are split into subsets and models are retrained on the combination of subsets to isolate and eliminate certain data. The approach suggested by Bourtoule et al. [1] involves splitting the dataset into chunks and retraining on each of the chunks, which is efficient. Nevertheless, the method involves the careful tuning of hyperparameters such as the number of shards and the process of data slicing. Conversely, other new approaches, including the one presented in our work, do not require any kind of hyperparameter scaling. As a case in point, Xu et al. [25] proposed the DeltaGrad algorithm, which uses the information available in the cache following a series of training steps to update the model and not initialize it afresh. This saves on computational load and allows for rapid adaptation. Knowledge distillation (KD) is another important concept that can be used to facilitate machine unlearning. KD, a model by Nguyen et al. [26], is a model compression method in which a smaller student model is trained to approximate the behavior of a larger teacher model. Cha et al. [29] took this notion and applied the ensemble methods to improve the student model. With respect to machine unlearning, one may retrain a student model on the remaining data after the deletion request with the assistance of KD. The student is also conditioned to follow the teacher (the original model without the lost information) so that a successful transfer of knowledge is achieved but not the information that is not needed. Model retraining, however, normally requires the reconstruction of the model wholly through the use of just preferred data. Although this ensures that there is no influence on the target data, it is computationally intensive and cannot be applied at a large scale. Machine unlearning is a more effective and scalable alternative because it applies the same effect at a lower cost and training time.

2.5 NAIVE UNLEARNING APPROACHES

In machine learning, a field undergoing rapid changes, unlearning has become important, especially with regard to data privacy and model adaptability. The basic methods used in this field, naive unlearning methods, target the elimination of certain data samples of trained models but do not require the entire retraining of the system. This becomes especially relevant in situations where the data had to be erased to adhere to applicable law or to make the ethical aspects of using the data smoother. These naive approaches usually involve simple approaches, for example, weight modification or selective retraining, to estimate the impact of eliminating particular data cases. They are not complex to execute; however, their effectiveness and efficiency may be different, depending on the model architecture behind them as well as the complexity of the data they operate with. This introduction discusses the principles, methodologies, and implications of the naive approaches to unlearning, preconditioning a more in-depth discussion of its strengths and weaknesses in the context of machine learning practices. In the weight adjustment method, the parameters are reset in the model to indicate a lack of certain data. Cha et al. suggested an approach named instance-wise unlearning [26]; it adjusts the weights of the model so that it can simulate the impact of distorting the training instances by dropping them. This method can be used to unlearn effectively without involving complete retraining. Selective retraining focuses on the reexamination of only the affected parts of the model. Xhu et al. investigated an unlearning technique in neural networks, in which network retraining is performed selectively; that is, only the data layers affected by the removal of particular data points are retrained. This reduces the rate of computation, but at the same time, the model can adjust properly to the changes. Naive unlearning mechanisms are the simplest and first approaches that aim to eliminate information that has been learned in machine learning models. Such mechanisms are mostly aimed at retraining the model afresh when certain data points are deleted. On the surface, such a strategy can be said to be logically correct, since the model will simply ignore any effect of the data that are deleted, since it will be exposed to the rest of the training samples. Nevertheless, its conceptual simplicity makes retraining a computationally intensive and ineffective task, especially in the age of massive datasets and deep neural networks. In practice, retraining is not a practical solution to any of these regularly changing or dynamic data settings, such as personalized recommender systems or real-time analytics platforms, where models need regular updates [3]. Naive unlearning (see Figure 2.2) does not fundamentally address privacy or compliance problems related to incomplete data deletion or vulnerabilities in data reconstruction. Although transient data points are not the subject of the retraining process, they do not provide any verifiable assurances that all the remaining evidence of the data has been successfully removed from the model, particularly with the possibility of using intermediate artifacts such as logs, caches, or support datasets. This lack of verifiable assurances is a major drawback where the data privacy law requires the right to be forgotten in the algorithm decision-making framework [4]. Therefore, although it forms the basis of the discussion on machine unlearning, the naive retraining–based solution is frequently used as a baseline or control group but not an actual or implementable solution to real machine learning pipelines today.

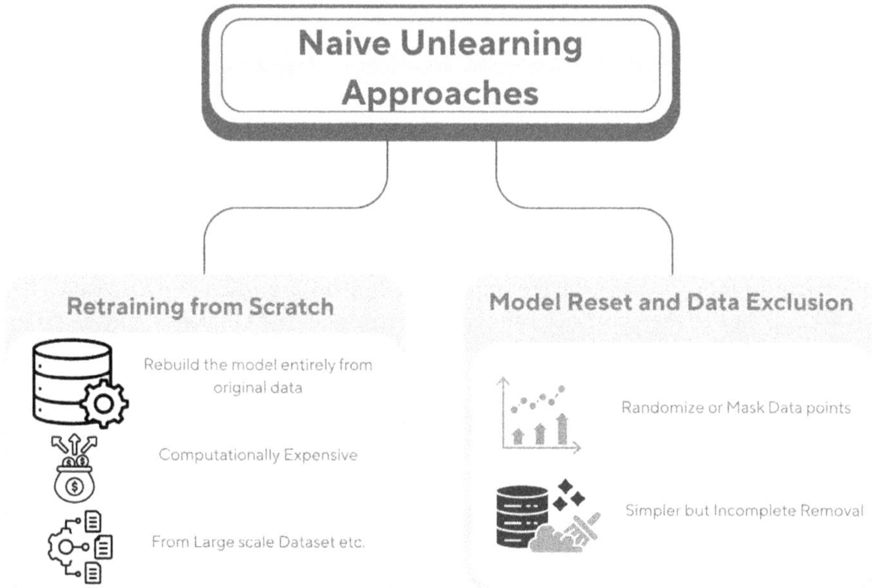

FIGURE 2.2 Naive unlearning approaches.

The other naive but widely used method in the field of naive unlearning is the method of data masking or perturbation. In this technique, rather than retraining the model completely, the data points to be deleted are subtly adjusted or randomized to remove the original effect of the data on the model to become statistically insignificant. Considering an example, adversarial noise may be introduced to the features or labels of a data point in a way that will cause disturbance to the predictive contribution. However, these measures [4] are rather complex than remedial. They do not guarantee actual unlearning, as the altered data still live through the training corpus, and the residual effect can still be transferred to the learned weights or decision boundaries of the model. Such techniques do not scale well to complex networks such as deep convolutional networks or transformers, where the data dependencies are not trivial and are highly entrenched in a series of nonlinear transformations. Such models being opaque also makes it more complex to verify that the data have indeed been erased, which is a crucial need in audit compliant systems. In addition, masking methods threaten to deteriorate performance on downstream tasks by causing noise and decreasing data quality and hence limiting generalizability. These trade-offs render naive perturbation strategies inappropriate for high-stakes applications such as healthcare diagnostics or autonomous driving, where the integrity of the learning process implemented by the model is the most crucial. Such unlearning approximations are impractical even at the theoretical level in low-resource or experimental contexts and fall short of the robustness, verifiability, and efficiency standards of industrial-scale AI deployments.

A similar naive algorithm involves altering or pruning network parameters under the assumption that model weights that are almost tied to particular points in the data can be changed or eliminated to allow forgetting. Overall, this approach would assess the value of a given case in the parameters of the model and, accordingly, undermine this impact through subtractive adjustments [1] or weight decays. Although this method of approach is intuitively good, it is fraught with practical difficulties. First, accurate estimation of the parameter effect of each of the data points is computationally expensive and is not consistent across multiple training runs because of stochastic initializations and optimization behaviors. Second, the neural networks of today are highly overparameterized and redundant; that is, the same ability to predict could be shared by a number of paths through the network. Therefore, the removal of a subset of parameters or the reweighting of a set will not necessarily fully remove the influence of the data, particularly in more advanced layers. In addition, the relationships between data samples as they are trained are nonlinear and complex; hence, cascading effects arise when selective forgetting is attempted without retraining globally. This algorithm also does not work well in sustaining post-unlearning performance because general pruning may cause performance deterioration or instability. Finally, these strategies usually do not have formal structures to offer demonstrable assurances of utter forgetting and hence are inadequate to satisfy regulatory measures. Consequently, although parameter-centric naive unlearning can be a computationally less intensive alternative to complete retraining, it is unreliable and erasure cannot be verified in the case of real-world applications that involve strict data privacy compliance.

Among the major constraints of naive unlearning methods is their failure to be generalized to other forms of learning, including supervised learning, unsupervised learning, and reinforcement learning. The most naive approaches have been formulated and experimented under the small scale in the supervised learning setup, specifically classification on curated images, such as the modified National Institute of Standards and Technology database or the Canadian Institute for Advanced Research [5]. However, in practice, heterogeneous types of data, multiple modes, and complicated feedback are common phenomena for which naive unlearning strategies are poorly prepared. As an example, in a reinforcement learning setting, the effect of a given data point cannot be explicitly observed as it diffuses via state transitions and compounding reward schemes. Similarly, the implicit training data representation of the training data in generative models, such as generative adversarial networks or variational autoencoders, ensures that direct removal is not a trivial task. Naive approaches in such environments not only localize data representations but also corrupt learned representations across the world, thus reducing model quality. The problem of scaling remains a bottleneck for naive solutions. Not only do industrial datasets of a large scale tend to be large, but they are dynamic, constantly changing, being added to and deleted. The training or trimming per deletion request is a source of significant maintenance overhead and is economically and operationally unsustainable. Such inefficiencies have prompted researchers to discover more advanced and adaptive machine unlearning methods such as certified removal, knowledge distillation-based unlearning, and ensemble-based forgetfulness protocols. These sophisticated schemes are aimed at providing measurable assurances of data elimination and keeping to a minimal level of computational load, thus overcoming the shortcomings of naive ones. In short, naive unlearning approaches have been used to provide initial understanding of the unlearning paradigm; however, these approaches lack the robustness, scalability, and compliance required in modern AI ecosystems.

2.5.1 Retraining from Scratch

The simplest and most conceptually explanatory approach to machine unlearning is retraining afresh. In this method, on a request to delete data, be it because of privacy regulations, a user withdrawing their permission or because of internal data handling policies, the whole machine learning model is thrown away, and the original data are then trained once more, without that data point. This approach ensures that the eventual model parameters are not directly exposed to the removed information, provided that there is no residual effect in ancillary data, for example, logs, caches, or random seed settings. In theory, retraining is the gold-standard point of reference with regard to achieving total and irreparable forgetting [3]. Since the data under consideration are never a part of the retraining process, the given approach, in accordance with the goal of forgetting, inherently meets the principles that are stipulated in the regulations related to data protection, such as the GDPR and CCPA. Nonetheless, the practical feasibility of this approach is in doubt because of its computing expense and lack of efficiency regarding modern deep learning frameworks, which are trained on datasets on the terabyte or larger range. The retraining process may require hours, days, or even weeks because of the complexity of the model and infrastructure and is therefore impossible for use in real-time systems, as well as in any other situation where deletion requests occur frequently or where the time constraints are critical. Other issues associated with the retraining-from-scratch paradigm include scalability and resource optimization, which are essential to industrial and research applications that work on large and dynamic datasets. In practice, datasets are seldom fixed, as new data are constantly being added, and users can be deprived of permission at any time. Complete retraining on individual deletion requests is operationally and economically forbidden. In even those cases where the batch deletions are aggregated and processed in periods, the level of computational cost will be significant. Furthermore, retraining is not readily compatible with existing machine learning pipelines, which focus on continuous learning, updating models, and deploying them in real time. Edge-deployed models and online learning systems, for example, cannot support frequent restarts and data resets.

Training involves the original data (without the examples that were deleted) being available in full, which is not always true because of storage capacity or data management rules. This creates another dimension of complexity regarding data retention and compliance, particularly when the training data are sourced at different locations or processed in federated nodes. Additionally, retraining does not consider the specifics of intersample relationships. The effect of a single data point can also spill over to adjacent samples in some operations because of similarity of features or correlation, and the deletion of a point can have a ripple effect on the statistical distribution of the training data. This interdependence also adds to the fact that retraining provides a clean, modular remedy to forgetting. Survey-wise, retraining afresh has typically served as a control in empirical tests of unlearning algorithms. More recent approaches, including knowledge distillation unlearning, projection-based forgetting, or SISA training [31], are generally compared to retraining-from-scratch paradigms according to the preservation of accuracy, the effectiveness of forgetting, and computational cost. Retraining offers the most forgetful fidelity in any comparison, yet it is extremely expensive in terms of resource utilization and time. It is an important tool in the evaluation of the performance of approximate or accelerated unlearning algorithms but is never considered a deployable solution outside of controlled, low-scale applications. Interestingly, retraining [6] is also a problematic issue in terms of the philosophy and methodology of machine unlearning. This causes the community to ask the question of whether unlearning should necessarily seek to achieve a level of perfect deletion fidelity or whether approximate and verifiable deletion with quantifiable assurances might be a more practical goal. Since machine unlearning is still developing into a separate subfield that cuts across privacy, security, and AI ethics, retraining is a necessary theoretical, yet seldom useful, device. Its value is therefore twofold: it provides a precise definition of what perfect unlearning may imply; it shows the inefficiencies and constraints fostering the pursuit of more scalable, flexible, and demonstrably safe options.

2.5.2 Model Reset and Data Exclusion

A trade-off between the simplicity of naive retraining and the growing need to have scalable and responsive unlearning methods is often put forward by mixing model reset and data exclusion. This approach fundamentally begins with the assumption that the presence of data to be forgotten can cause the existing model to be unreliable. The system in turn responds to this by initiating a reset, retraining a new model on only the remaining, accepted data, and dropping the existing model state. To reduce the load, the model reset often relies on modular components or preserved architectures instead of pure retraining-from-scratch approaches, which may need full replication of the original training environment and data. This design has become common, particularly in data-driven systems whose user consent policies evolve over time, and developers need an operation shortcut to delete particular data influences without interruption [3]. The advantage of this method is its clarity. It is a simple concept; delete the data, reinitiate the model, and begin a new with only the now permitted data. This has consequences as far as legal compliance is concerned. Although regulatory systems such as the California Consumer Privacy Act and the GDPR do not imply how unlearning is supposed to be performed, they emphasize that the request of the data subject should be followed. Model reset methods have a clear audit trail with a known point of reset and a corresponding snapshot of the data that proves the absence of data. Owing to this fact, many firms whose work processes are sensitive to privacy have begun to adopt some forms of this method as an interim measure as they seek alternative unlearning mechanisms that are more sophisticated. Although it seems to be simple in nature, there are nuances in the interaction between model reset and different learning scenarios. A full reform might lead to a system that is dependent on adaptive updating or continuous learning becoming disrupted. Reinitiating such systems may result in a major loss of valuable model behavior, which could cost a substantial amount of time and resources to reinitiate. These systems are based on the long-term maintenance of learned representations. An example would be regularly resetting personalized recommendation engines that change on a day-to-day basis with constant opt-outs or deletion requests. Even the partial loss of historical behavioral patterns may affect system performance and user satisfaction considerably. These trade-offs point to a deeper tension between the desire to retain the learned value and successful unlearning, which cannot be easily resolved with the help of resets alone.

The exclusion process and reset procedure are more complex in distributed/federated learning environments. As the data that must be forgotten may be distributed among multiple client devices, an organized model reset may not be possible or may be prohibitively costly to initiate. Various copies of the training data can exist on each node, and simple exclusion can be complicated to interpret because of the interdependencies brought about by the combination of models during training. To make matters worse, single users can desire to have their data deleted as the system continues to learn with others. This requires selective forgetting but does not interfere with the communal structure of the entire structure. Model reset can be applied in such cases quite often as a final option, and it can be applied only internationally when it is legally necessary rather than a routine procedure. The operations on auxiliary components—features of the training environment or processes that may survive beyond the main model file—are critical considerations that should be considered during model reset. A few examples of these are optimizer states, data logs, checkpointed weights, and meta-learning configurations. Unless these artifacts are deleted during a reset of the model, there is a probability that the deleted data may indirectly affect the model behavior. Adam or SGD optimizers, such as those storing momentum or dynamically changing learning rate histories, often do not reset these factors to zero; without resetting them, there is a risk that the retrained model will be implicitly biased. Thus, to ensure the integrity of a model reset, it is necessary to not only remove data in the training set but also ensure that the full state of computation of the model and its environment is reset in some manner. One of the most captivating issues of recent research is the possibility of modular reinitialization or partial resets. The entire model is not discarded; only a part of the model is affected: generally the layers that are nearest to the input and that form data-specific representations. This selective reset technique is meant to balance data exclusion and performance preservation. It is theoretically promising, but it may be difficult to see what layers or components to reset without deep analysis of the impact of the data. A single piece of data can affect a number of parameters across a deep network, making targeted forgetting inaccurate unless it has been established with high-quality attribution tools. Researchers are exploring techniques such as influence functions and gradient attribution to identify which features of the model are the most influenced by certain data points [7]. Nevertheless, these efforts are immature and are not powerful enough to be used in high-stakes cases.

What makes a model reset with data exclusion an interesting research topic is its symbolic value. It summarizes the initial difficulties in the machine learning community in finding a balance between the temporality of data ownership and the permanence of learned representations. In traditional statistical modeling, datasets are fixed and very rare after training models are updated. In addition to being responsive, adaptive, and customized, learning systems today need to be reversible, interpretable, and compliant. The given dichotomy contrives a design quandary: to wear models deliberately to forget, or to always have to start over. The latter tends to occur more often in the case of model reset. It is a brute-force approach that offers operational simplicity to prevent complexity. Nevertheless, the need for smarter, more efficient, and verifiable unlearning will increase only because of alterations in data regulations and the increase in awareness among users. Ethical and emotional aspects should also be taken into account. From one perspective, when a model is reconfigured to erase the data of a given individual, it is an outright acceptance of the agency of this individual and the fact that the model has no knowledge that was acquired from that individual. This gesture may not appear to be highly technical, but with regard to the sociotechnical world, it underscores the importance of user rights in the machine learning process. Model reset procedures help researchers and developers remember that data are not isolated. It is responsible and forgets an obligation, especially in systems that grow more intelligent, and is a moral and legal obligation, even though it is technically challenging. In summary, data exclusion and model reset remain important not only as unlearning tools but also as measures of the accountability redesign of AI systems. Despite their practical restrictions, which restrict their applications in dynamic or distributed environments, they offer clarity and compliance. More advanced techniques that can produce certified removal, targeted forgetting, or knowledge distillation could become popular for replacing reset techniques. Nevertheless, they are likely to continue to be a safety net and a reference point, an obvious, although costly, way of a sure route to ensure that data truly have been forgotten.

2.6 APPROXIMATE UNLEARNING METHODS

Responsible data management is becoming increasingly important as machine learning models become increasingly involved in decision-making in sectors such as healthcare, finance, and surveillance (Figure 2.3). Despite the use of naive unlearning methods, such as retraining or model reset, ensuring compliance with requests related to data deletion by completely deleting and rebuilding models, these methods are computationally expensive, operationally infeasible, and unsupported by modern unwound AI systems. This bottleneck of operation is leading to the increased popularity of approximate unlearning methods (see Figure 2.3). These methods do not require full retraining and are used to remove or reduce the effects of specific training data on the models. The primary objective is to develop efficient algorithms that, without deteriorating the respectable performance and privacy standards, are able to recreate the impact of retraining with the deleted data. These approaches aim to achieve a trade-off to provide a provable or empirically substantiated approximation of deletion, which is less expensive, faster, and more scalable than are the other strategies, without yielding complete forgetting. Imprecise methods will become more significant as machine unlearning progresses, particularly in environments where timely, auditable, and verifiable unlearning will be more valuable than theoretical

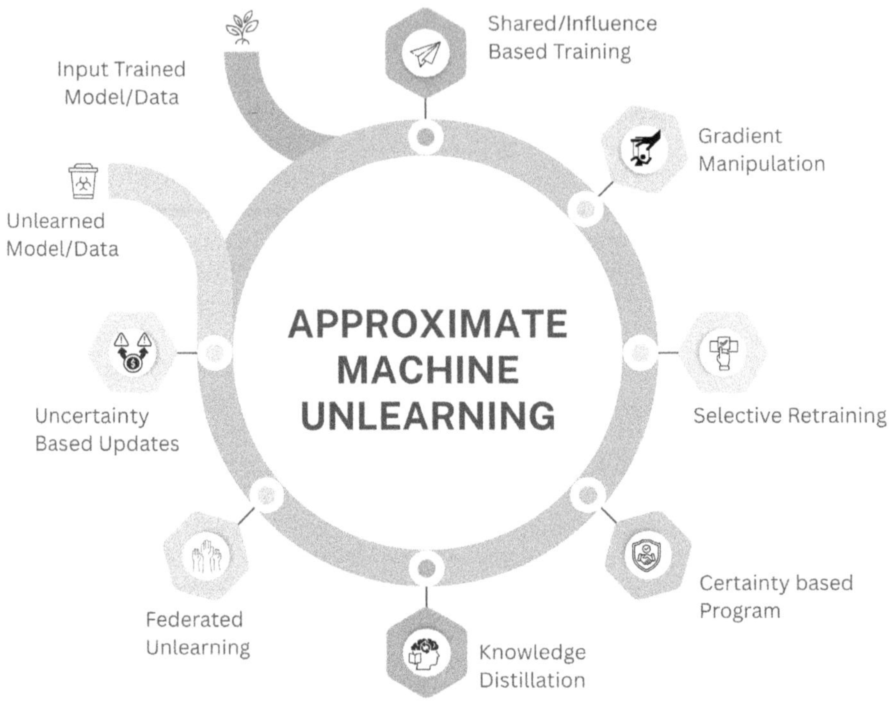

FIGURE 2.3 Approximate unlearning methods.

perfection. A primary factor that contributes to the interest in approximate unlearning is the increasing complexity of the models themselves. Recurrently retraining deep learning models of this type is impossible because these models often contain millions or even billions of parameters because they are deep learning models. One of the early frameworks to explore this concept was SISA [1], which was suggested by Bourtoule et al. The training data are further divided into small segments used in the isolated model training in SISA, with each of the disjoint shards further split into segments. The slices containing only the target piece of data have to be retrained in response to a deletion request; the resulting partial models can be reaggregated. This allows efficient deletion of the entire model without recomputing the whole model and reduces the total relearning burden. SISA provides an effective starting point on which most of the other approximation algorithms are found even though it is not capable of guaranteeing perfect forgetting, especially when the effect of the erased data spreads across slices. Another strategy familiar in the context of approximate unlearning is influence-based unlearning. These methods often rely on the concept of perturbation theory or classical statistics to identify the extent to which a given point of training affects the model parameters or predictions. Of special importance is the role played by the function framework [7] developed by Koh and Liang. Influence functions allow the model to estimate influence on the basis of the gradient and the Hessian of a point on the data to approximate the gradient on the basis of the influence and the Hessian to determine the influence on the gradient. To generate the effect of unlearning the data point without retraining, the idea of unlearning is to compute the inverse of this effect and add it to the model parameters. Although it is elegant, this method has a disadvantage because it is based on assumptions regarding the convexity and smoothness of models, and these assumptions are not always applicable in modern deep networks. Moreover, estimating Hessians (or their inverses) at scale is computationally expensive (particularly when large models are used). Despite these issues, influence-based techniques offer interpretability and finer control; therefore, they are suitable in a scenario where auditing and understanding the effects of data points are as important as removing them. Innovation in approximate unlearning has also been brought about by the application of gradient manipulation and parameter correction techniques. These techniques operate in the parameter space of the trained model, attempting to counteract or attempt to undo the effect of certain data by acting on the gradient of the parameter space over the training set. To remove data effects, researchers have attempted to walk the model backward in parameter space by subtracting the gradient of a data point into the model [10].

Although gradient-based correction does not require the use of second-order derivative approximations, it is conceptually similar to influence functions. However, in practice, it is often challenging to apply these techniques to nonconvex environments, where there is a vast disparity between local minima and where the training path is path dependent. Since the ultimate condition of the model can be the result of a complicated connection between a vast number of training samples, it is difficult to isolate the influence of a data point from a single model. They become even more difficult in adaptive optimizers such as Adam or root mean square propagation (RMSProp), where the momentum and learning rate history influence the convergence behavior. Nevertheless, gradient correction has demonstrated potential in providing deletion effects with little retraining in the context of controlled tasks such as image classification and small natural language processing (NLP). One approach to approximate unlearning that has become more inventive and popular is knowledge distillation. In this paradigm, a student model is learned to imitate the behavior of a teacher model, however, only when working with the data on which deletion targets have been filtered out. In this way, the output behavior of the original model is relearned, which is not subject to the influence of the forgotten data. The distillation process [32] is a lossy compression of knowledge that is useful for minimizing memory and computational overhead. It also introduces a kind of abstraction that impairs the input of individual data points, which helps them to unlearn. A significant strength of unlearning based on distillation is that it can be reconfigured into a new model or even integrated into a whole new system, which essentially performs a soft reset of the original model, which is not being retrained. Nevertheless, distillation is approximate in nature. Even the student model may still remain with remnants of the forgotten information in case it was confounded by the teacher's predictions. The effectiveness of the strategy is determined by the quality of the teacher products and fidelity of the distillation process. However, in numerous practical scenarios, primarily in resource-constrained environments, knowledge distillation provides a successful trade-off between performance, unlearning accuracy, and scalability.

Different types of approximate unlearning approaches are dedicated to selective retraining. Rather than retraining an entire model or performing abstract parameter corrections, these methods update only those components of a model that have been most impacted by the data to be dropped, for example, certain layers or weights. An example in convolutional neural networks is layer-wise retraining, where the data-less sensitive layers are frozen, followed by retraining only the first or middle layers, where the representation is most data specific [9]. This focused unlearning is capable of minimizing computational expenses and maintaining the general performance of the model in addition to eliminating meaningful effects on the eliminated data. Nonetheless, the choice of success of such strategies strongly relies on the architecture and the ability to properly isolate the data influence. Deep networks are more likely to confound representations, and it is difficult to determine which components of the model are actually specific to the data.

There is a risk of either inadequate forgetting or unnecessary loss of performance as a result of selective retraining when there are no reliable attribution devices. Federated unlearning is a new technique that integrates distributed learning structures with selective retraining. Federated models are trained together and do not centralize raw data, and the data of each user remain on his or her local device in federated environments. Since end users can delete their local data and retrain or modify their local models without retraining the entire global system, it presents a particular advantage in unlearning. The central model can be updated with the help of an aggregation round that does not encompass the users that are affected. Therefore, if the underlying aggregation and communication protocols are designed to support such updates, then compared with centralized approaches, federated unlearning could prove better and be more privacy aware [11]. However, this method also has its disadvantages, especially in ensuring that updates do not reintroduce data that have been deleted by using correlated users or model parameter estimates that are old. Therefore, studies in this area have concentrated on mechanisms such as secure aggregation and differential privacy, which provide credible assurances of unlearning in addition to effective deletion. Approximate unlearning is also interfaced with uncertainty estimation. To quantify the uncertainty caused by deleting specific data points, researchers have proposed the use of dropout-based ensembles or Bayesian neural networks. The objective is to selectively update parts of the model that are significantly perturbed and monitor the development of model confidence when the data are deleted. This probabilistic method of unlearning makes a softer concept of deletion in which the impact of data is described as a distributional shift that can be reversed over time instead of a presence or absence. These are methods whose experimental stages have yet to be tested, but these methods give the path to the joint action of continual learning systems that adapt intuitively to the alterations in the data together with approximate unlearning. Approximate unlearning also has several disadvantages. It is by definition cognizant of the fact that the model might also have a trace of the data that have been lost. This tension is problematic in situations where deletion is not only a desirable but also a necessary action. To ensure compliance in controlled environments such as legal or financial applications, approximation methods should be backed by intensive certification/verification systems. Recently, formal verification methods of unlearning, where algorithms not only attempt at forgetting but also produce some measurable signs of forgetting, such as predictive alignment metrics or divergence scores have been created [29]. These tools facilitate the transparency and reliability of approximate unlearning since they bridge the gap between accountability and efficiency. Approximate unlearning techniques that embody a realistic response to the surging needs of data deletion in AI systems are presented as a practical solution. They offer resource-efficient and scalable variants that enable systems to react to dynamic data policies without undergoing a prohibitive retraining price, although they may not provide flawless forgetting. These methods demonstrate that unlearning does not necessarily involve starting over, with knowledge distillation, gradient reversals, slicing-based training, influence functions, or selective retraining. Unlearning, which is likely to be an essential component of the responsible use of machine learning models, will likely be approximate when learning becomes increasingly advanced in research and models become more refined and have more practical applications. To be successful, it must be closely incorporated with system design, regulatory compliance, and societal expectations of digital rights and autonomy in addition to algorithmic innovation.

2.6.1 Fine-Tuning and Gradient Reversal

Fine-tuning is a transfer learning approach in which an already trained neural network is then trained on a reshaped dataset to train its internal parameters without corrupting already acquired general representations. Fine-tuning is often applied in machine unlearning, where the impact of certain instances is minimized without necessitating the rest of the model to be retrained. Cevallos et al. established that fine-tuning-based unlearning algorithms [12] should be designed to update the weights related to specific samples in a balance between forgetting and model usefulness. Nonetheless, more recent findings indicate that naive or under-constrained fine-tuning can still leave harmful information that adversarial or data-poisoning environments cannot remove [14]. Adaptive gradient-based updates have been suggested as adaptive optimization strategies that can enhance efficiency and stability in selective forgetting [15]. These methods optimize gradient updates to reduce residual images of the deleted data and do not impair the predictive accuracy on the retained datasets.

Gradient reversal is an adversarial training process that seeks to encourage representation invariance by flipping gradients at backpropagation. This method is typically realized by a gradient reversal layer, which is a combination of gradient multiplication by a negative scalar, which encourages the feature extractor to obtain uninformative embeddings with respect to a given attribute. Gradient reversal in machine unlearning may be used to suppress representations related to data that are to be removed by adversarial training of a discriminator to identify these representations and at the same time require the encoder to conceal them. Zhang et al. proved that adversarial [16] and contrastive objectives may optimize the difference between forgotten and retained data distributions, which is useful for strengthening forgetting. However, as noted by Pawelczyk et al., some unlearning strategies [14] still have residual vulnerability, particularly to poisoning attacks. Thus, gradient-based adversarial mechanisms are additional technologies to complementary technologies in more comprehensive unlearning to reinforce selective data deletion.

2.6.2 Knowledge Distillation and Substitution

Knowledge distillation has become a utility-preserving and structured method of machine unlearning where knowledge stored in a teacher model is transferred to a student model without information related to the data to be removed. Rather than learning model parameters directly, distillation learns to produce the distribution of outputs of the teacher on the held-out data and absorbs undesired knowledge indirectly. Kim et al. suggested selective knowledge distillation [32] in which the retained decision behavior is transferred to a soft decision tree, which allows interpretable and controlled forgetting. Similarly, Zheng et al. presented graph unlearning using knowledge distillation [33], where a student graph model undergoes retraining to copy a sanitized teacher by essentially eliminating the impact of deleted nodes or edges without disrupting structural consistency. These methods indicate that the sensitive information and generalizable patterns in distillation can be decoupled, which is a scalable alternative to full retraining and can reduce computational costs.

Knowledge substitution builds on the paradigm of distillation by substituting or recreating representations on the basis of the forgotten information and not just inhibiting it. In this environment, the components whose outputs are affected by the targeted samples are retrained with alternative signals or adjusted at the adversarial layer with straightened layers. Kim et al. (2024) proposed layer attack unlearning [30], a synthesis of layer-based perturbation and knowledge distillation that can be used to perform faster forgetting but at the same time maintain accuracy and show that layer-specific substitution can be both efficient and precise. Parallel evidence from systematic studies focuses on the fact that even complementary strategies with regard to substitution can address the reduction in performance, which is typically experienced in unlearn strategies that are naive by rebalancing internal representations rather than creating informational gaps [17]. Knowledge distillation and substitution are combined to create a hybrid unlearning model: distillation transfers benign predictive behavior, and substitution recreates or modifies components of the affected system to generate robust, efficient, and utility-aware machine unlearning.

2.7 EXACT UNLEARNING METHODS

The goals of exact unlearning techniques are to ensure that a trained model acts in the same way as a model that is retrained without the deleted data. These methods offer formal assurances that the effect of particular samples is entirely eliminated as opposed to being suppressed in an approximate fashion. As an example, fast exact unlearning algorithms to learn in context with LLMs analytically deactivate the contribution of particular demonstrations without retraining [18]. These guarantees are reinforced by certified frameworks, which add some statistical validation or hypothesis testing mechanisms to ensure that deleted samples no longer modify model behavior [19, 22]. Gaussian-certified unlearning is used to make probabilistic guarantees in the high-dimensional setting that the trained model is distributionally equal to its retrained counterpart [22]. Privacy-sensitive or regulatory practices, where provable compliance is needed, are particularly sensitive to such certified and analytically based approaches.

Recent studies have generalized precise unlearning to larger and more complicated environments. Group-robust unlearning algorithms address fairness and subgroup consistency by ensuring that the deletion is not highly impacted by a particular demographic or structural group [20]. In multimodal LLMs, single-image unlearning models have been utilized effectively and yield accurate or almost accurate elimination of visuals without incurring any harm to linguistic functions [34]. Extensive surveys emphasize that although exact unlearning has the best theoretical guarantees, it can have high computational and implementation complexity in comparison with approximate variants [24]. In high-stakes settings, which demand provable privacy, regulation, or adversarial resistance, however, precise algorithms are usually preferred over approximate ones, and guarantees are more important than their low computational efficiency.

REFERENCES

1. Bourtoule, L., Chandrasekaran, V., Jia, H., Travers, A., Zhang, B., Evans, D., & El Ghaoui, L. (2021). Machine unlearning. Proceedings of the IEEE Symposium on Security and Privacy, 141–159. https://doi.org/10.1109/SP40001.2021.00038
2. Garg, A., Singhal, P., Kaushik, S., & Mittal, S. (2020). Right to be forgotten: A privacy perspective under GDPR. International Journal of Law and Information Technology, 28(3), 221–240. https://doi.org/10.1093/ijlit/eaaa002
3. Ginart, A., Guan, M. Y., Valiant, G., & Zou, J. (2019). Making AI forget you: Data deletion in machine learning. Advances in Neural Information Processing Systems (NeurIPS), 32.
4. Sekhari, A., Rajput, S., Dagan, Y., & Thakurta, A. (2021). Remember what you want to forget: Algorithms for machine unlearning. arXiv preprint arXiv:2109.05976. https://arxiv.org/abs/2109.05976
5. Schelter, S., Gade, S., Götzfried, J., Harth, A., & Anderson, M. (2021). A practical guide to machine unlearning. Proceedings of the VLDB Endowment, 14(12), 2701–2704. https://doi.org/10.14778/3476311.3476376
6. Golatkar, A., Achille, A., & Soatto, S. (2023). Mixed signals: Toward practical private unlearning in deep neural networks. Proceedings of the IEEE/CVF Conference on Computer Vision and Pattern Recognition (CVPR), 11245–11254. https://doi.org/10.1109/CVPR52729.2023.01044
7. Koh, P. W., Sagawa, S., Marklund, H., Xie, S. M., Zhang, M., Balsubramani, A., Hu, W., Yasunaga, M., Phillips, J., Gao, I., & Liang, P. (2019). Understanding black-box predictions via influence functions. Proceedings of the International Conference on Machine Learning (ICML), 1885–1894.
8. Mehta, A., Zhang, R., Neel, S., Roth, A., & Thakurta, A. (2022). A theoretical investigation of machine unlearning. Proceedings of the 39th International Conference on Machine Learning (ICML), 16082–16089.
9. Izzo, C., Blaas, A., Bellet, A., & Malek, M. (2021). Approximate unlearning with feedback. arXiv preprint arXiv:2112.09122. https://arxiv.org/abs/2112.09122
10. Neel, S., Roth, A., & Wu, Z. S. (2022). Descent-to-delete: Gradient-based methods for machine unlearning. arXiv preprint arXiv:2207.07544. https://arxiv.org/abs/2207.07544

11. Yin, Z., Sharma, Y., Mo, Y., & Guha, S. (2023). FedEraser: Enabling efficient user-level data removal from federated learning models. Proceedings of the 2023 ACM SIGSAC Conference on Computer and Communications Security (CCS), 456–468. https://doi.org/10.1145/3576915.3623122
12. Cevallos, I. D., Benalcázar, M. E., Valdivieso Caraguay, Á. L., Zea, J. A., & Barona-López, L. I. (2025). A systematic literature review of machine unlearning techniques in neural networks. Computers, 14(4), 150. https://doi.org/10.3390/computers14040150
13. Goel, S., Prabhu, A., Torr, P., Kumaraguru, P., & Sanyal, A. (2024). Corrective machine unlearning. arXiv preprint arXiv:2402.14015.
14. Pawelczyk, M., Di, J. Z., Lu, Y., Kamath, G., Sekhari, A., & Neel, S. (2024). Machine unlearning fails to remove data poisoning attacks. arXiv preprint arXiv:2406.17216.
15. Ghannam, N. E., & Mahareek, E. A. (2025). AGU: Adaptive gradient unlearning for efficient machine unlearning. Intelligent Systems with Applications, 28, 200592. https://doi.org/10.1016/j.iswa.2025.200592
16. Zhang, Q., Yang, C., Lou, J., & Xiong, L. (2024). Contrastive unlearning: A contrastive approach to machine unlearning. In Proceedings of the Thirty-Fourth International Joint Conference on Artificial Intelligence (IJCAI-25) (pp. 7464–7472). arXiv:2401.10458.
17. Cevallos, I. D., Benalcázar, M. E., Valdivieso Caraguay, Á. L., Zea, J. A., & Barona-López, L. I. (2025). A systematic literature review of machine unlearning techniques in neural networks. Computers, 14(4), 150. https://doi.org/10.3390/computers14040150
18. Muresanu, A. I., Thudi, A., Zhang, M. R., & Papernot, N. (2024). Fast exact unlearning for in-context learning data for LLMs. arXiv preprint arXiv:2402.00751.
19. Martínez Llamas, J., Preuveneers, D., & Joosen, W. (2025). Certified unlearning for a trustworthy machine learning-based access control administration. International Journal of Information Security, 24, 94. https://doi.org/10.1007/s10207-025-01003-5
20. De Min, T., Roy, S., Lathuilière, S., Ricci, E., & Mancini, M. (2025). Group-robust machine unlearning. arXiv preprint arXiv:2503.09330.
21. Xu, H., Zhu, T., Zhang, L., Zhou, W., & Yu, P. S. (2023). Machine unlearning: A survey. ACM Computing Surveys, 56(1), Article 9, 1–36. https://doi.org/10.1145/3603620
22. Pandey, A., Auddy, A., Zou, H., Maleki, A., & Kulkarni, S. (2025). Gaussian certified unlearning in high dimensions: A hypothesis testing approach. arXiv preprint arXiv:2510.13094.
23. Cao, Y., & Yang, J. (2015, May). Toward making systems forget with machine unlearning. In 2015 IEEE Symposium on Security and Privacy (pp. 463–480). IEEE.
24. Xu, J., Wu, Z., Wang, C., & Jia, X. (2024). Machine unlearning: Solutions and challenges. IEEE Transactions on Emerging Topics in Computational Intelligence, 8(3), 2150–2168.
25. Nguyen, T. T., Huynh, T. T., Ren, Z., Nguyen, P. L., Liew, A. W. C., Yin, H., & Nguyen, Q. V. H. (2025). A survey of machine unlearning. ACM Transactions on Intelligent Systems and Technology, 16(5), 1–46.
26. Cha, S., Cho, S., Hwang, D., Lee, H., Moon, T., & Lee, M. (2024, March). Learning to unlearn: Instancewise unlearning for pretrained classifiers. In Proceedings of the AAAI Conference on Artificial Intelligence (Vol. 38, No. 10, pp. 11186–11194).
27. https://www.bitraser.com/article/DoD-5220-22-m-standard-for-drive-erasure.php?srsltid=AfmBOoom2uhHMvJyT-eWDwnftpIDnkH9OqLvZrMXg5JOaORW5dh_kc0N
28. Kissel, R., Regenscheid, A., Scholl, M., & Stine, K. (2014). Guidelines for media sanitization (NIST Special Publication 800-88 Revision 1). National Institute of Standards and Technology. https://doi.org/10.6028/NIST.SP.800-88r1

29. Gupta, V., Jung, C., Neel, S., Roth, A., Sharifi-Malvajerdi, S., & Waites, C. (2021). Adaptive machine unlearning. Advances in Neural Information Processing Systems, 34, 16319–16330.
30. Kim, H., Lee, S., & Woo, S. S. (2024). Layer attack unlearning: Fast and accurate machine unlearning via layer level attack and knowledge distillation. In Proceedings of the AAAI Conference on Artificial Intelligence (Vol. 38, No. 19, pp. 21241–21248).
31. Koch, K., & Soll, M. (2023, February). No matter how you slice it: Machine unlearning with sisa comes at the expense of minority classes. In 2023 IEEE Conference on Secure and Trustworthy Machine Learning (SaTML) (pp. 622–637). IEEE.
32. Kim, S., Lee, B., Park, S., Lee, M., & Rho, S. (2025). A framework for machine unlearning using selective knowledge distillation into soft decision tree. Annals of Computer Science and Information Systems, 45, 95–101.
33. Zheng, W., Liu, X., Wang, Y., & Lin, X. (2023). Graph unlearning using knowledge distillation. In International Conference on Information and Communications Security (pp. 485–501). Springer Nature Singapore.
34. Li, J., Wei, Q., Zhang, C., Qi, G., Du, M., Chen, Y., . . . Liu, F. (2024). Single image unlearning: Efficient machine unlearning in multimodal large language models. Advances in Neural Information Processing Systems, 37, 35414–35453.

3 Machine Unlearning in Generative AI and LLMs

3.1 OVERVIEW OF UNLEARNING CHALLENGES IN GENERATIVE AI AND LLMS

Large language models (LLMs) can be made to unlearn: to selectively remove certain learned information—personal data, copyrighted material, harmful behavior, or systemic biases—without retraining the entire system to new values. This functionality has gained greater relevance because of legal factors such as the right to be forgotten, privacy standards, and ethical concerns in the implementation of AI [1, 2]. It is difficult to directly apply the original machine unlearning algorithms, which are designed to perform classification, to generative LLMs because of the large sizes of their parameter space, open-ended outputs, and memories of intricate linguistic and factual structures. In addition, unlearning methods should be able to balance efficient forgetting and the maintenance of utility; excessive removal of target knowledge can negatively affect overall model performance, whereas more conservative approaches can preserve some residual information [2, 3]. This challenge is further complicated by access restrictions: most deployed LLMs are available only as black-box APIs, preventing the use of parameter-based unlearning and compelling people to use manipulations at inference times that only obstruct but do not remove learned knowledge [3]. There are a few fundamental challenges that are based on gaps in evaluation and robustness. To effectively gauge whether unlearning has actually eliminated specific knowledge in all its contextual and inferential aspects, existing indicators tend to overestimate forgetting through a limited focus on direct performance decline [1]. Additionally, unlearning methods have robustness problems; for example, adversarial methods or quantizing the model can reconstruct the information that was previously forgotten, or otherwise undo unlearning, revealing that weight or representation manipulation can be counterproductive to forgetting [2, 4]. Unlearning is also complicated by ethical and governance considerations: it is necessary to decide not only what should be unlearned but also how to balance competing values (e.g., copyright vs. freedom of expression) and how to incorporate human-in-the-loop controls, which adds additional complexity that cannot be addressed by purely technical solutions alone.

3.2 UNLEARNING IN GENERATIVE AI

In generative artificial intelligence (GenAI), unlearning is the process of removing particular training data effects on pretrained models in a manner that does not require retraining of the entire model. Generative models, which are based on approximations of complex probability distributions [5–7] on high-dimensional data, are unlike

DOI: 10.1201/9781003771470-3

classical supervised learning. Formally, a generative model learns parameters (θ) that maximize the likelihood:

$$\theta^{*} = \text{argarg}\sum\nolimits_{(x,y)\in D} \text{loglog}\, P_{\theta}\left(x\right) \tag{1}$$

where D represents the training dataset. When a subset $\left(D_{f} \subset D\right)$ must be forgotten, the objective of unlearning is to approximate parameters $\left(\theta^{-f}\right)$ such that the model behaves as if it were trained on $\left(D \setminus D_{f}\right)$ [6]. However, because generative models encode distributed representations, removing the contribution of D_f without affecting general knowledge remains highly nontrivial.

Current approaches to unlearning in generative AI fall into two major categories: parameter modification and inference-time intervention. Parameter-based methods attempt to minimize the influence of forgotten data through additional optimization, often framed as shown in equation (3.2):

$$L_{\text{retain}}\left(\theta\right) + \lambda L_{\text{forget}}\left(\theta\right) \tag{3.2}$$

where L_{retain} preserves the performance on the retained data and L_{forget} penalizes the memorization of D_f with λ controlling the forgetting strength [5]. Although they are efficient, the methods can result in performance degradation or forget incompleteness because of residual parameter interactions. In contrast, in-context unlearning changes prompts or decoding strategies to eliminate unwanted outputs; however, it does not imply the removal of underlying learned representation [5]. Evaluation and reversibility are crucial problems in generative unlearning. According to recent research, surface-level output removal is not a guarantee of deleted latent representations; forgotten knowledge can be regenerated via adversarial prompts or minimal fine-tuning [6]. This phenomenon proves the assumption that parameter updates are equal to permanent deletion. Theoretically, the ideal unlearning needs are shown in equation (3.3):

$$P_{\theta^{-f}}\left(x\right) \approx P_{\theta^{\setminus f}}\left(x\right) \tag{3.3}$$

where $\left(\theta^{\setminus f}\right)$ denotes parameters obtained by full retraining without D_f. This equivalence at scale is still computationally impossible for modern LLMs and multimodal generative systems [5, 7].

Apart from technical impediments, governance and compliance issues also make generative unlearning more complex. Regulatory requirements such as the right to erasure require verifiable guarantees, but the definition of measurable conditions of complete forgetting in probabilistic models remains open to definition [5]. Generative systems that operate in public spaces have to strike a balance between privacy, fairness, and creative integrity. During the further growth of generative AI to applications with high impact, verifiable, robust, and computationally efficient unlearning mechanisms will be needed to provide trust, accountability, and long-term sustainability [5, 7]. The various unlearning methods of unlearning in generative AI (see Figure 3.1) are discussed next.

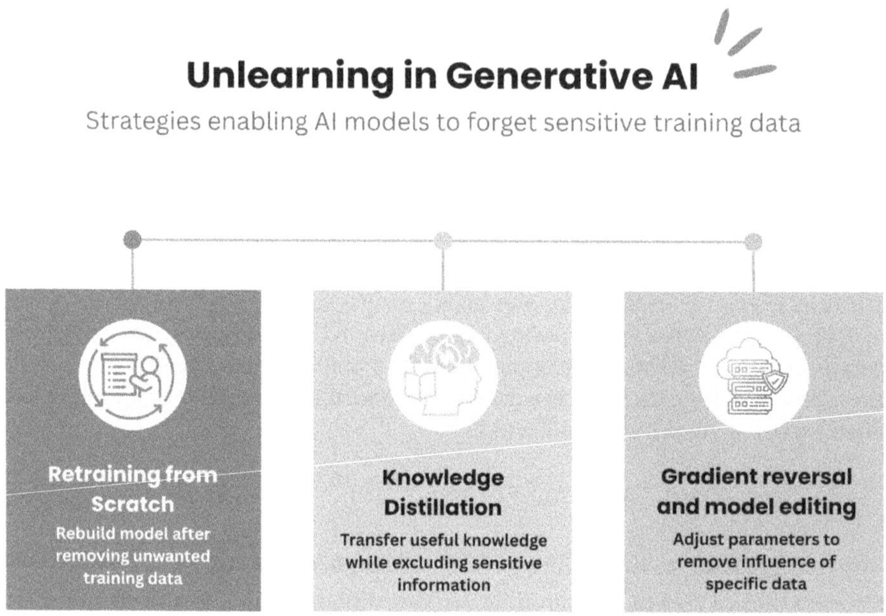

FIGURE 3.1 Unlearning in generative AI.

3.2.1 Retraining from Scratch

The best way to guarantee that information in particular data points is completely removed in a trained machine learning model is to retrain the model using a fresh set of data (also known as exact unlearning). Formally, given a training dataset D and a subset D_f to remove, retraining from scratch aims to compute new parameters θ_r using the learning algorithm as shown in equation (3.4):

$$\theta_r = A\left(D \setminus D_f\right) \tag{3.4}$$

This ensures that the resultant model will behave as it would have behaved had the removed data not been shown to it, meets the strictest understanding of unlearning, and meets regulatory requirements such as the right to erasure. It is computationally expensive and impractical with large models such as deep neural networks or generative models trained on large-scale datasets, as millions of GPU hours and much energy may be needed to train a model. Recent theoretical studies emphasize that even the ideal goal of retraining equivalence is essentially difficult to accomplish in modern training pipelines, particularly for LLMs. In multistage models (e.g., pre-training and fine-tuning), the result of the local unlearning process [8, 9] depends on the order of training stages; thus, it is mathematically impossible to have simple unlearning updates to rediscover the distribution of a model that is retrained with a fresh start on all the possible training paths. These observations indicate that precise retraining is not only costly but also conceptually inappropriate for staged training.

Nevertheless, despite these difficulties, retraining afresh provides a background against which approximate unlearning techniques are compared. Approximate techniques—such as influence-function adjustments or sharded retraining—aim to *minimize deviations* from the retrained model's behavior, often measured by distributional distances such as the Kullback–Leibler divergence $D_{KL}\left(P_{\theta_u} \| P_{\theta_r}\right)$, where θ_u denotes [10, 11] the unlearned model's parameters. These methods balance efficiency and fidelity but still fall short of the theoretical guarantees offered by full retraining, especially in high-stakes applications involving generative AI and data privacy.

3.2.2 Knowledge Distillation

Knowledge distillation (KD) [12] is a transfer-learning framework in which a compact student model S learns to approximate the behavior of a larger teacher model T. Originally proposed for model compression, KD has become a powerful mechanism for efficient machine unlearning. The standard objective minimizes the divergence between teacher and student predictive distributions using softened logit, as given in equation (3.5):

$$L_{KD} = T^2 D_{KL}\left(p_T^{(T)}(y \mid x) \| p_S^{(T)}(y \mid x)\right) \quad (3.5)$$

where T is the temperature parameter controlling distribution smoothness. In unlearning settings, distillation allows the student to inherit retained knowledge from the teacher while selectively excluding information associated with data designated for deletion [13, 14].

In machine unlearning, KD is adapted to explicitly separate retained and forgotten knowledge. Approaches such as *distill to delete* decompose representations so that the student minimizes influence from deleted samples while preserving task-relevant performance [14]. This is often implemented through a composite objective as given in equation (3.6):

$$L = L_{\text{retain}} + \lambda L_{\text{forget}} + \beta L_{\text{KD}} \quad (3.6)$$

where L_{retain} preserves accuracy on the remaining data, L_{forget} penalizes the dependence on the deleted samples, and L_{KD} ensures alignment with the teacher's retained knowledge. This mechanism is further optimized by decoupled distillation frameworks, which hide or separate logits akin to deletion targets, which allows targeted forgetting without complete retraining [15]. These structured distillation models require fewer computations than a retraining scheme that trains the model entirely does, but the model utility remains competitive.

Recent developments have investigated proven and partitionalized distillation mechanisms that have provided theoretical assurances of unlearning fidelity. To illustrate, ensemble-based distillation models divide teacher influence in such a way that in the event of deletion, the components of the students that are affected need to be retrained, which allows retraining to be more cost-effective and retraining-equivalent behavior to be approximated [13]. Nonetheless, there are still concerns with residual information leakage and adversarial probing robustness, particularly in large generative models. Knowledge distillation is therefore a computationally efficient but an inaccurate substitute for precise retraining, trading off scalability, fidelity, and regulatory compliance [13, 16].

3.2.3 Gradient Reversal and Model Editing

Gradient reversal techniques are employed to mitigate the influence of undesirable patterns in machine learning models—such as bias or unwanted information—by augmenting the training objective with adversarial objectives. Originally introduced in domain adaptation, gradient reversal layers [17] invert gradients for specific components during backpropagation, effectively training the model to *forget* certain features while preserving overall task performance. Mathematically, if L_{task} is the primary task loss and L_{rev} is the loss for the adversarial component, the gradient reversal computation is given in equation (3.7):

$$\theta \leftarrow \theta - \eta\left(\nabla_{\theta} L_{\text{task}} - \lambda \nabla_{\theta} L_{\text{rev}}\right) \tag{3.7}$$

where λ controls the strength of the reversal. In unlearning, this mechanism can be adapted to suppress representations directly tied to data or attributes designated for removal, allowing targeted forgetting without full retraining [17, 18].

Model editing extends this idea by directly modifying internal model parameters to correct or erase specific learned behaviors. Instead of globally retraining, editing techniques perform minimal, localized updates—often at the level of specific neurons or layers—guided by gradient signals that isolate the influence of unwanted content. This can be framed as a constrained optimization problem, as shown in equation (3.8):

$$min_{\Delta\theta} \| \Delta\theta \|^2 \ s.t. f_{\theta+\Delta\theta}\left(x_u\right) = y_{\text{target}} \tag{3.8}$$

where x_u are inputs [18] associated with undesirable behavior and y_{target} is the desired corrected output. Such edits aim to preserve global function f_θ elsewhere while eliminating undesired responses [19, 20]. Recent research emphasizes the fact that gradient reversal and model editing can be effective approximations to more expensive unlearning algorithms and allow selective adjustments to be made at reduced computational cost. Nevertheless, robustness and unwanted side effects remain issues, as reversed gradients or edits can unintentionally worsen performance on retained items or create residual latent data. It is also an ongoing research topic in machine unlearning and the application of AI ethically to ensure that the process of editing generalizes to generalized cases and that when applied to other parts of the model, it does not cause unwanted behavioral transfer [17, 21].

3.3 UNLEARNING IN LLMS

In the context of LLMs, unlearning is the ability to selectively eliminate specific learned information—for example, sensitive personal data, copyrighted text, or dangerous biases—without much loss in useful general performance. Targeted forgetting is especially difficult since unlike the old-fashioned unlearning of the classification task, LLMs unite information in extensive corpora and distributed parameter space. The objective is often framed as modifying the model parameters θ to obtain θ^{-f}such that the model behaves as if it were retrained without the deleted data subset D_f, as given in equation (3.9):

$$P_{\theta^{-f}}\left(y \mid x\right) \approx P_{\theta^{\backslash f}}\left(y \mid x\right) \tag{3.9}$$

where $\theta^{\backslash f}$ denotes parameters from full retraining without D_f. Achieving this equivalence is computationally infeasible for large models, and many unlearning strategies focus on approximations that balance forgetting with intact performance [22, 23].

Recent studies have emphasized (see Figure 3.2) that such a naive deactivation of direct links with forgotten information frequently does not destroy latent representations, allowing unlearning whereby forgotten data can be remembered by probing or fine-tuning. This finding reveals that apparent forgetting, which is indicated by a lower probability of particular tokens, is not similar to the actual removal of hidden knowledge. Research focuses on more rigorous measures of evaluation, which investigate the dynamics of internal representation and alignment spaces to better estimate unlearning efficacy. Consequently, embedding-level interventions, adversarial training, and constrained fine-tuning are being increasingly studied by unlearning methods as the means to modify the behaviors of LLMs without requiring complete retraining [24, 25].

Several algorithmic approaches to LLM unlearning have been suggested, such as embedding-corruption prompts, which impose forgetting constraints in inference, and robust elastic models, which maximize forgetting under adversarial settings.

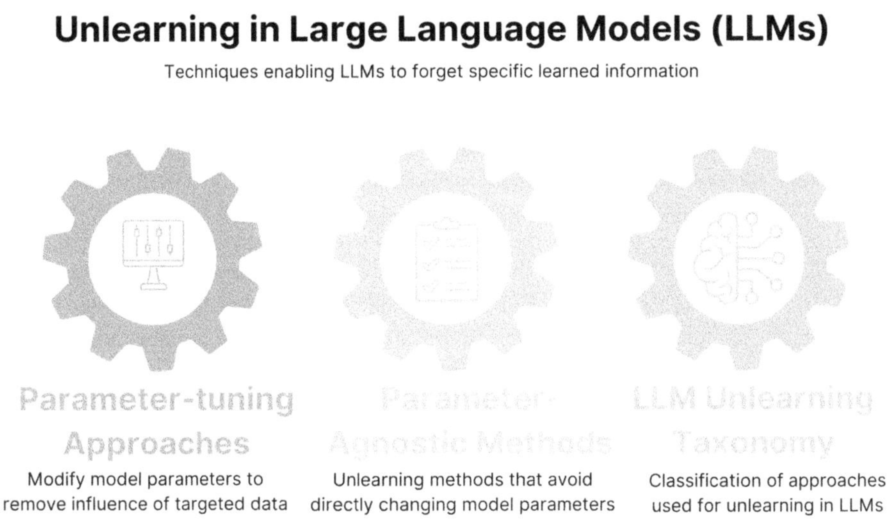

FIGURE 3.2 Unlearning in LLMs.

The objectives of these approaches are to eliminate the power of the specific data and still be useful for the remainder of the model; however, they are only approximate. An increasing interest is also in verifiable unlearning, in which models can provide evidence of irreversibility and resistance to the revival of deleted knowledge. With the implementation of LLMs in sensitive systems related to privacy, compliance, and ethics, scalable and certifiable mechanisms of unlearning will be critical in generating confidence in generative AI systems [22–25].

3.3.1 Parameter-Tuning Approaches

With respect to machine unlearning, there are parameter-tuning approaches to unlearning that work to remove the effects of particular training cases by simply altering the learned weights rather than retraining them. Sharma and Jha [26] introduce effective unlearning using weight tuning and residual regularization whereby the specific parameter adjustments are confined so that the original solution is not too far away and the contributions of the forget set are learned. It is also a very large-scale deep neural network strategy since it minimizes the number of computations and does not require complete optimization cycles. This scheme uses a combination of fine-tuning of models through controlled mechanisms, gradient reweighting, and loss correction to ensure that the model mirrors behavior as although it has been trained without the removed data. This process is further refined by influence-guided updates of the parameter, which approximates how the model parameters are sensitive to particular training samples. Liu, Zhang, and Wang [27] use influence functions and second-order approximations to determine the parameters that are most significant in terms of encoding some information in the forget set. Selective control over these high-impact weights can suppress residual memorization without losing the knowledge that is retained. Nguyen et al. [28] built upon this concept by introducing powerful parameter update models that use stability-related requirements and adversarial robustness tests to avoid overforgetting or performance decline. These algorithms are usually combinations of regularization terms, Fisher information-based penalties, and localized sparsity constraints that enable the updates to be localized in the parameter space.

Hearings carry out evaluation studies that provide insight into the strengths and limitations of parameter-tuning approaches. Chen and Zhao [29] prove that effective forgetting can be implemented at much lower retraining costs, although in this way, representation entanglement in deep models may be detected by probing attacks. Patel, Singh, and Lee consider the trade-off between utility retention and forgetting fidelity, offering multi-objective optimization solutions that trade-off between predictive accuracy, robustness, and compliance and data deletion requests. Taken together, these works put parameter tuning as a scalable and feasible unlearning mechanism, but issues of verification, residual leakage, and theoretical guarantees are active research topics.

3.3.2 Parameter-Agnostic Methods

The term "parameter-agnostic unlearning" describes methods that seek to eliminate the effect of certain training data without involving a process of parameter adjustment of a machine learning model or a complete retraining of the model. In contrast to parameter-tuning algorithms, which vary internal weights or gradients, parameter-agnostic algorithms are insensitive to the structure of the parameters of a model and thus are generalized across architectures and tasks. A notable category of these methods is model-agnostic unlearning, which can be used with any learning algorithm and can be said to be resistant to the details of the representation of knowledge inside the model. They are especially useful in situations where manipulating or reading model parameters is not feasible, for example, in large pretrained models deployed in APIs. Data transformation and perturbation constitute one set of parameter-agnostic methods in which the training data or unlearning request is data transformed prior to or after training to remove a sensitive example. Methods such as differential privacy add controlled noise to either training or data to guarantee that the removal of a single point has a limited impact on the model behavior, providing statistical assurance of the broadcast of individual data without the need to modify parameters. The other is model-agnostic scoring and example weighting, where the significance of the training samples is estimated and deemphasized using loss reweighting or data filtering, practically making the model less dependent on the data points at which the unlearning is aimed. These methods are aimed at regulating the functions of data influence at the dataset level but not altering the learned representation itself.

Recent studies have also suggested superior frameworks that improve parameter-agnostic unlearning through architectural and algorithmic development. For example, geometric routing invariance preservation is an algorithm-insensitive unlearning approach to mixed-of-experts models that limits router functions, decouples routing behavior and expert parameter updates, and imposes structural forgetting instead of weight updates. Task-neutral gradient models use adaptive gradients that do not need task-specific tuning or understanding of parameter values, making it possible to apply unlearning at scale even when unlearning ratios are very large by applying gradient flow at a more abstract level instead of directly working with the actual weight values. Although parameter-agnostic methods are widely applicable, they have issues such as being complete to unlearn and being verifiable. Since they do not directly change the way information is encoded in model parameters, residual influence might be present in latent representations and can be retrieved during adversarial probing or membership inference attacks. However, parameter-agnostic approaches offer scalable, flexible unlearning that can be deployed in specific deployments, particularly where parameter access is restricted and model architectures are heterogeneous, because those methods do not rely on internal model specification.

3.3.3 LLM Unlearning Taxonomy

Unlearning in LLMs has quickly become a narrow specialty of machine unlearning because of the distinct demands of data privacy, ethical compliance, and harmful-behavior mitigation in generative AI [30, 31]. In contrast to conventional unlearning, which is formulated to support only simple classifiers, LLM unlearning has to contend with large parameter space, distributed, entangled knowledge representations that themselves make it particularly difficult to perform targeted forgetting [22, 23].

To structure the approaches in this space, recent surveys suggest taxonomies, that is, classification of the unlearning methods, by their technical mechanisms and objectives of unlearning. LLM unlearning algorithms can be classified into three general categories of algorithms: parameter modification, input modification, and robust unlearning. Parameter modification methods are methods that explicitly adjust the weights or network variables of a model to eliminate the effects of unwanted data, typically by making use of gradient-based adoptions, model editing, or auxiliary variables called security vectors to guide the model to undesirable behavior. Prompt manipulation techniques, such as in-context unlearning, manipulate inputs without any reference to internal parameters and thus are more appropriate for black-box deployment but do not provide a high probability of forgetting [22]. A third category, robust unlearning, places greater emphasis on adversarial attack and jailbreaking vector resistance through the introduction of adversarial training and threat-conscious evaluation into the unlearning process as an acknowledgment of the unlearning process being irreversible and secure as well as effective [22]. Other taxonomic models focus on intention and outcome. As an example, certain works draw the distinction between methods that attempt to remove true internal knowledge and those that simply attempt to repress behavioral expressions of that knowledge without altering latent representations—a very critical difference, as superficial suppression can be overcome with only a small amount of fine-tuning or probing, as demonstrated in representation studies of unlearning reversibility [23–25]. These taxonomies are useful for understanding the implicit assumptions underlying various unlearning strategies, points of evaluation failure (e.g., benchmarking diversity and robustness metrics), and future research directions to create scalable, verifiable, and ethically justified unlearning methods for generative LLMs.

3.4 COMPARATIVE INSIGHTS

Unlearning LLMs [26, 27] constitute a new subdiscipline that aims to selectively delete specific knowledge about an object while maintaining the overall performance of the generative systems and fulfilling privacy and safety standards.

The methods in this area have been proposed as taxonomies that are defined according to the location and mode of unlearning interventions: training-time (parameter modification), posttraining (parameter pruning and editing), and inference-time (input or prompt-based methods) [22]. Table 3.1 provides a comparison between typical frameworks and research directions in generative AI and unlearning using LLM, demonstrating differences in the models used, the results obtained, and gaps in the research that still exist. Frameworks that modify parameters modify weights or model architectures to remove undesired information, and inference-level methods modify prompts to affect results without altering internal representations. A portion of the literature focuses on effective unlearning [28, 29], that is, the processes that are meant to withstand adversarial attacks and verification threats not only by forgetting but also by providing security and reliability. Assessment taxonomies also differentiate measures of forgetting quality, utility maintenance, robustness, and efficiency, reflecting the multifacetedness of the measurement of the performance of unlearning.

TABLE 3.1
Comparison of LLM Unlearning Frameworks

Author	Title of Work	Models Used	Outcome	Research Gap
Le-Khac and Truong (2025) [22]	LLM unlearning taxonomy	Survey	Taxonomy of unlearning categories	Evaluation benchmarks
Geng et al. (2025) [27]	Survey of LLM Unlearning	LLMs (general)	Structured overview	Deep benchmarks
Qiu et al. (2025) [5]	LLM Unlearning Survey	Survey	Pipeline taxonomy	Metric diversity
Yao et al. (2024) [29]	Machine Unlearning of Pretrained LLMs	Pretrained LLMs	Efficiency benchmarks	Large scale tasks
Si et al. (2023) [3]	LLM Unlearning Objectives	Transformers	Defined objectives	Robustness metrics
Xu et al. (2025) [8]	Unlearning Isn't Deletion	GPT-style	Reversibility analysis	Latent leakage
Pawelczyk et al. (2023) [32]	ICUL: In-context Unlearning	LLM QA models	Prompt-based forgetting	Forgetting guarantee
Bhaila et al. (2024) [33]	SPUL Soft Prompting	LLMs	Prompt optimization	Robust adversarial forgetting
Sheshadri et al. (2024) [34]	Latent Adversarial Unlearning	LLMs	Enhanced robustness	Deployment tests
Zhang et al. (2024) [35]	Safe Unlearning Framework	LLMs	Offset model unlearning	Black-box settings
Huang et al. (2024) [36]	δ-UNLEARNING	LLMs	Logit offsets	Utility preservation
Ji et al. (2024) [37]	ULD Unlearning	LLMs	Baseline comparison	Standardized evaluation
Lu et al. (2025) [38]	Detox Unlearning	Align LLMs	Toxicity suppression	Generalization
Yuan et al. (2025) [39]	Robust Unlearning	LLMs	Adversarial resistance	Scalability
ACL Anthology (2024) [29]	Pretrained LLM Unlearning	Multiple LLMs	Efficiency metrics	Large benchmarks

REFERENCES

1. Blanco-Justicia, A., Jebreel, N., Manzanares-Salor, B., Sánchez, D., Domingo-Ferrer, J., Collell, G., & Tan, K. E. (2025). Digital forgetting in large language models: A survey of unlearning methods. *Artificial Intelligence Review*, *58*(3), 90. https://doi.org/10.1007/s10462-024-11078-6

2. Kang, J. J., Bui, D., Pham, T., & Ling, H.-C. (2025). *Unlearning imperative: Securing trustworthy and responsible LLMs through engineered forgetting.* arXiv. https://doi.org/10.48550/arXiv.2511.09855
3. Si, N., Zhang, H., Chang, H., Zhang, W., Qu, D., & Zhang, W. (2023). *Knowledge unlearning for LLMs: Tasks, methods, and challenges.* arXiv. https://doi.org/10.48550/arXiv.2311.15766
4. Lizzo, T., & Heck, L. (2026). *Unlearning in LLMs: Methods, evaluation, and open challenges.* arXiv. https://doi.org/10.48550/arXiv.2601.13264
5. Qiu, R., Tan, J., Pu, J., Wang, H., Gao, X.-S., & Sun, F. (2025). *A survey on unlearning in large language models.* arXiv. https://doi.org/10.48550/arXiv.2510.25117
6. Bourtoule, L., Chandrasekaran, V., Choquette-Choo, C. A., Jia, H., Travers, A., Zhang, B., . . . & Papernot, N. (2021). Machine unlearning. *IEEE Symposium on Security and Privacy.* https://doi.org/10.1109/SP40001.2021.00014
7. Liu, Z., Dou, G., Tan, Z., Tian, Y., & Jiang, M. (2024). *Machine unlearning in generative AI: A survey.* arXiv. https://doi.org/10.48550/arXiv.2407.20516
8. Xu, X., Yue, X., Liu, Y., Ye, Q., Hu, H., & Du, M. (2025). *Unlearning isn't deletion: Investigating reversibility of machine unlearning in LLMs.* arXiv. https://doi.org/10.48550/arXiv.2505.16831
9. Shumailov, I., Hayes, J., Triantafillou, E., Ortiz-Jimenez, G., Papernot, N., Jagielski, M., & Bagdasaryan, E. (2024). *Unlearning: Unlearning is not sufficient for content regulation in advanced generative AI.* arXiv. https://doi.org/10.48550/arXiv.2407.00106
10. Wang, W., Tian, Z., Zhang, C., & Yu, S. (2024). *Machine unlearning: A comprehensive survey.* arXiv. https://doi.org/10.48550/arXiv.2405.07406
11. Li, C. (2025). *An overview of machine unlearning.* ScienceDirect.
12. Yu, J., He, Y., Goyal, A., & Arora, S. (2025). *On the impossibility of retrain equivalence in machine unlearning.* arXiv.
13. Quan, Y., Li, Z., & Montana, G. (2025). *Efficient verified machine unlearning for distillation.* arXiv. https://doi.org/10.48550/arXiv.2503.22539
14. Sinha, Y., Mandal, M., & Kankanhalli, M. (2023). *Distill to delete: Unlearning in graph networks with knowledge distillation.* arXiv. https://doi.org/10.48550/arXiv.2309.16173
15. Zhou, Y., Zheng, D., Mo, Q., Lu, R., Lin, K.-Y., & Zheng, W.-S. (2025). *Decoupled distillation to erase: A general unlearning method for class-centric tasks.* arXiv. https://doi.org/10.48550/arXiv.2503.23751
16. Cevallos, I. D., Benalcázar, M. E., Valdivieso-Caraguay, Á. L., Zea, J. A., & Barona-López, L. I. (2025). A systematic literature review of machine unlearning techniques in neural networks. *Computers, 14*(4), 150. https://doi.org/10.3390/computers14040150
17. Zhang, Y., Gan, C., Xu, Z., & others. (2024). *Toward efficient unlearning via gradient reversal and adversarial objective adaptation.* arXiv. https://doi.org/10.48550/arXiv.2406.09391
18. Cevallos, I. D., Benalcázar, M. E., Valdivieso-Caraguay, Á. L., Zea, J. A., & Barona-López, L. I. (2025). A systematic literature review of machine unlearning techniques in neural networks. *Computers, 14*(4), 150. https://doi.org/10.3390/computers14040150
19. Mitchell, M., et al. (2023). *Model editing for safer and correctable AI.* OpenReview. https://openreview.net/forum?id=iKqQGEOeej
20. Ahmad, M. A., et al. (2024). Bias removal techniques in machine learning using gradient reversal. *Applied Sciences, 13*(16), 9341. https://doi.org/10.3390/app13169341
21. Wang, W., Tian, Z., Zhang, C., & Yu, S. (2024). *Machine unlearning: A comprehensive survey.* arXiv. https://doi.org/10.48550/arXiv.2405.07406
22. Le-Khac, U. N., & Truong, V. N. X. (2025). A survey on large language models unlearning: Taxonomy, evaluations, and future directions. *Artificial Intelligence Review.* https://doi.org/10.1007/s10462-025-11376-7

23. Geng, J., Li, Q., Woisetschlaeger, H., Chen, Z., Cai, F., Wang, Y., Nakov, P., Jacobsen, H.-A., & Karray, F. (2025). *A comprehensive survey of machine unlearning techniques for large language models.* arXiv. https://doi.org/10.48550/arXiv.2503.01854
24. Qiu, R., Tan, J., Pu, J., Wang, H., Gao, X.-S., & Sun, F. (2025). *A survey on unlearning in large language models.* arXiv. https://doi.org/10.48550/arXiv.2510.25117
25. Liu, C., Wang, Y., Flanigan, J., & Liu, Y. (2024). *Large language model unlearning by embedding-corrupted prompts.* NeurIPS Poster. (Available on NeurIPS 2024 virtual proceedings)
26. Le-Khac, U. N., & Truong, V. N. X. (2025). A survey on large language models unlearning: Taxonomy, evaluations, and future directions. *Artificial Intelligence Review.* https://doi.org/10.1007/s10462-025-11376-7
27. Geng, J., Li, Q., Woisetschlaeger, H., Chen, Z., Cai, F., Wang, Y., . . . & Karray, F. (2025). *A comprehensive survey of machine unlearning techniques for large language models.* arXiv. https://doi.org/10.48550/arXiv.2503.01854
28. Qiu, R., Tan, J., Pu, J., Wang, H., Gao, X.-S., & Sun, F. (2025). *A survey on unlearning in large language models.* arXiv. https://doi.org/10.48550/arXiv.2510.25117
29. Yao, J., Chien, E., Du, M., Niu, X., Wang, T., & Yue, Z. (2024). Machine unlearning of pretrained large language models. *ACL Anthology.* https://aclanthology.org/2024.acl-long.457
30. Zhou, J., Li, T., Fong, S. J., Dey, N., & Crespo, R. G. (2023). Exploring chatGPT'S potential for consultation, recommendations and report diagnosis: Gastric cancer and gastroscopy reports' case. *IJIMAI, 8*(2), 7–13.
31. Khosravy, M., Gupta, N., Dey, N., & Witkowski, O. (2025, February). Are LLMs Ready to Shoulder Biomedical Trust? In International conference on innovations in biotechnology and health sciences (pp. 125–142). Singapore: Springer Nature Singapore.
32. Pawelczyk, Martin, Seth Neel, and Himabindu Lakkaraju. (2023). "In-context unlearning: Language models as few shot unlearners." arXiv preprint arXiv:2310.07579.
33. Bhaila, K., Van, M.-H., & Wu, X. (2024). Soft prompting for unlearning in large language models. arXiv. https://doi.org/10.48550/arXiv.2406.12038
34. Sheshadri, Abhay, et al. (2024). "Latent adversarial training improves robustness to persistent harmful behaviors in llms." arXiv preprint arXiv:2407.15549.
35. Zhang, Zhexin, et al. (2024). "Safe unlearning: A surprisingly effective and generalizable solution to defend against jailbreak attacks." arXiv preprint arXiv:2407.02855 1.2 (2024): 3.
36. Huang, James Y., et al. (2024). "Offset unlearning for large language models." arXiv preprint arXiv:2404.11045.
37. Ji, Jiabao, et al. (2024). "Reversing the forget-retain objectives: An efficient llm unlearning framework from logit difference." Advances in Neural Information Processing Systems 37 (2024): 12581-12611.
38. Lu, Yifan, et al. (2025). "Adaptive detoxification: Safeguarding general capabilities of LLMs through toxicity-aware knowledge editing." Findings of the Association for Computational Linguistics: ACL 2025.
39. Yuan, Hongbang, et al. (2025). "Towards robust knowledge unlearning: An adversarial framework for assessing and improving unlearning robustness in large language models." Proceedings of the AAAI Conference on Artificial Intelligence. Vol. 39. No. 24.

4 Benchmark Datasets and Experimental Frameworks

4.1 PUBLIC DATASETS FOR EVALUATING MACHINE UNLEARNING

As large language models (LLMs) have been rapidly advancing, multimodal large language models (MLLMs) have become influential systems capable of reasoning on several modalities, such as text and images. Although these models have achieved good success in multimodal use, they also pose serious privacy and security issues, as witnessed with LLMs. Machine unlearning (MU) is also complicated by the incorporation of multimodal data because sensitive information can be spread among various modalities. There are no well-established benchmarks or publicly available datasets for assessing MUs in MLLMs [1].

4.1.1 TOFU

The task of fictitious unlearning (TOFU) benchmark [2] consists of a synthetic set of factual information regarding fictitious authors and a fine-tuned large language model meta AI (LLaMA) on the same data. The goal is to forget information about a number of authors selectively and retain information about the remaining authors. In line with this, forget queries are limited to authors belonging to a forget set, and retain queries cover questions concerning the rest of the authors and the general world knowledge. As the data are completely composed, the sources of the unlearned targets are single and easy to distinguish, and they are not present in the pretraining data of the model. This design allows accurate and strong assessment of unlearning efficiency.

4.1.2 WMDP

The weapons of mass destruction proxy (WMDP) benchmark was presented to handle the shortcomings of current benchmarks [3]. It is composed of 3,668 meticulously edited multiple-choice questions and requires many resources to create. The WMDP is a proxy for the evaluation of dangerous knowledge with respect to biosecurity, cybersecurity, or chemical security. Two types of benchmark queries are used: benign (retain) queries and harmful (forget) queries, which allow the systematic measurement of the capacity of a model to erase dangerous knowledge while retaining safe and legitimate information [4].

 DOI: 10.1201/9781003771470-4

4.1.3 CIFAR-10

A popular example of data used in computer vision and machine learning research is Canadian Institute for Advanced Research (CIFAR-10) [5] data. It has 60,000 32×32 pixel color images of ten object types, of which 50,000 images are used for training and 10,000 for testing. The dataset is quite diverse, as it consists of a wide variety of everyday objects, and classifying an image is difficult. It is an ideal choice because of its balanced design and moderate complexity, which gives CIFAR-10 the ability to assess machine unlearning techniques that do not deteriorate as a whole model of the trained data.

4.1.4 MNIST

The modified National Institute of Standards and Technology (MNIST) [6] is a typical benchmark in the field of handwritten digit recognition, and it comprises 70,000 handwritten images of digits ranging between 0 and 9, with a resolution of 28×28 pixels. MNIST is a controlled environment for studying the basic behavior of unlearning algorithms, as it is simple and widely used in previous studies and makes it possible to evaluate their effectiveness without the help of any other visual complexity.

4.1.5 Fashion MNIST

MNIST was later challenged by fashion-MNIST [7]. It contains 70,000 grayscale images of fashion pieces of ten categories, including shirts, trousers, and sneakers, and the same number of grayscales as in MNIST. This is a more challenging classification task because of the greater visual diversity and ambiguity of the clothing items, which provides a more realistic point of reference concerning the strength of unlearning algorithms [8, 9].

4.1.6 UTKFace

UTKFace is a large-scale group of facial images with diverse ages, with a range between 0 and 116 years [10]. It consists of more than 20,000 age-, sex-, and ethnicity-annotated images and has significant variability in terms of pose, illumination, facial expression, occlusion, and resolution. This variety renders UTKFace appropriate for investigating machine unlearning with respect to sensitive tasks of facial analysis.

4.1.7 Machine Unlearning for Facial Age Classifiers

The Machine Unlearning to Facial Age Classification (MUFAC) dataset [11] was developed to test unlearning in the task of age estimation. For this benchmark, the original model uses multiclass classification and eight age categories, as each age category represents a particular age range. MUFAC makes it possible to systematically examine the ability of unlearning algorithms to deactivate age-related knowledge and maintain performance in the remaining classes.

4.1.8 Machine Unlearning for the Celebrity Attribute Classifier

The CelebA-based machine unlearning to attribute classification (Machine Unlearning for Celebrity Attribute Classification) benchmark [11] is a multilabel benchmark that uses binary attributes, that is, gender and age group. MUCAC allows the evaluation of the selective removal of sensitive attributes by adapting CelebA to unlearning conditions and sustaining predictive accuracy for nontarget attributes.

4.2 UNLEARNING-SPECIFIC BENCHMARKS

In addition to general-purpose datasets, various benchmarks have been created with a principled and application-oriented view of machine unlearning. These standards are concerned with the special needs of unlearning, for example, preserving privacy, removing selective knowledge, and maintaining the utility of a model over repeated unlearning requests.

4.2.1 Machine Unlearning Six-Way Evaluation

The machine unlearning six-way evaluation (MUSE) benchmark [12] offers an all-encompassing framework for evaluating the quality of unlearned models. Six desirable properties that an effective method of unlearning must meet are analyzed: (1) no verbatim memorization, (2) no memorization of knowledge, (3) privacy leakage is prevented, (4) utility is preserved on nonremoved data, (5) unlearning can be scaled with respect to the size of the requested unlearning, and (6) it can withstand unlearning in a series of operations.

MUSE is specifically focused on balancing both the owner of the data and the model deployers. With respect to the data owners, an unlearned model must not regurgitate the removed data verbatim; it must be unable to answer questions about the forgotten data, and it must not exhibit any sign that it is already trained on the removed data. MUSE provides a strict and comprehensive criterion for machine unlearning algorithm evaluation by combining privacy guarantees and deployment feasibility. Figure 4.1 shows the MUSE benchmark framework for evaluating unlearning model quality.

4.2.2 Real-World Knowledge Unlearning

The benchmark that is concerned with unlearning of factual knowledge on a real-world figure, such as Stephen King, is the real-world knowledge unlearning (RWKU) benchmark [13].

4.2.2.1 Forget Assessment

Forget assessment measures the performance of unlearning by assessing knowledge memorization and knowledge manipulation. In knowledge memorization, the question is whether the model can still remember information that it had received during the training period, and in knowledge manipulation, the question is whether

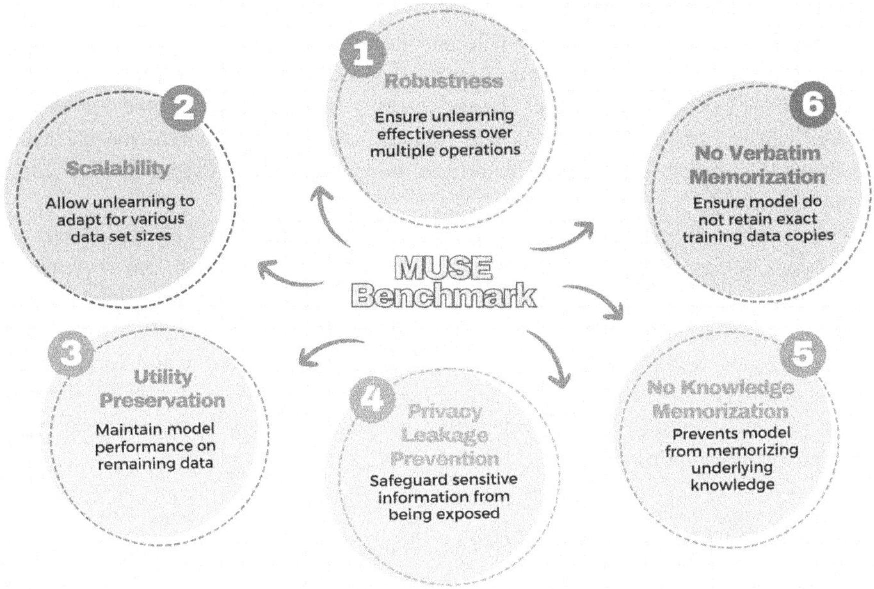

FIGURE 4.1 MUSE benchmark framework for evaluating unlearning model quality.

the model can use the information that it has learned in the downstream tasks. The higher-level reasoning and application of knowledge make knowledge manipulation a more rigorous requirement.

4.2.2.1.1 Knowledge Memorization

In the case of knowledge memorization, fill-in-the-blank probes are built using Wikipedia sentences that feature the unlearning targets, and the significant information is obscure. The ROUGE-L recall score is used to measure model performance, where low scores indicate more efficient unlearning. To identify any remaining knowledge further, membership inference attacks are used by comparing a forget member set and a retain member set. The higher LOSS scores of the forget member set than of the retain set indicate that the target knowledge has been removed, with LOSS scores primarily reported. Higher LOSS scores on the forget member than on the retain member indicate effective unlearning.

4.2.2.1.2 Knowledge Manipulation

Knowledge manipulation is assessed through question-answer probabilities that are based on paraphrasing and restructuring of facts that relate to the target. Several adversarial attack probes are introduced to simulate malicious attempts to retrieve forgotten information, such as role playing, synonym substitution, in-context learning, and cross-lingual querying. ROUGE-L recall is used to test both the standard and adversarial probes, and low scores indicate better unlearning.

4.2.2.2 Retain Assessment

Retain assessment is used to study whether the unlearning process undermines the initial abilities of the model. It focuses on two important issues, namely, locality and model utility. Locality guarantees that unlearning is limited to targeted knowledge without causing disturbances to closely related information, whereas model utility measures the ability of the model to remain unchanged with respect to other tasks in the real world.

The locality is tested through neighbor perturbation by testing the model on knowledge that is related but dissimilar to the unlearning targets. An increase in the scores signifies a more successful maintenance of adjacent knowledge. Model utility is evaluated with a set of standard benchmarks such as the MMLU on general ability, Big-Bench-Hard on reasoning, TruthfulQA on truthfulness, and TriviaQA on factuality and entropy measures to fluency via AlpacaEval. The overall effectiveness of the model is not affected by unlearning because of the consistent performance across these benchmarks.

4.3 UNLEARNING EFFICIENCY

Although the accuracy of forgetting is also important, the effectiveness of the unlearning mechanism is also critical to practice. In practice, models are often updated, and training a model again is often computationally infeasible. Therefore, determining the resource efficiency of unlearning methods is highly important. Experiments in the literature [14–18] usually evaluate unlearning efficiency on the basis of the speed of the unlearn, that is, the difference in time between the unlearn and naive retraining. A larger difference implies accelerated recovery of privacy, security, and model utility.

The time to unlearn is the simplest efficiency measure, as it reflects the amount of time it takes to go through the process of unlearning. The measure is especially pertinent in a large or controlled setting, that is, financial services, where noncompliance can result by delayed unlearning, leading to operational risk [19–21]. Methods such as approximate unlearning [22] and federated unlearning seek to reduce such time by training only those components of the model that are sensitive to the data to be deleted instead of training the whole model.

In addition to time, computational cost, which is a reflection of the hardware and energy consumed during unlearning, is a parameter. Large-scale models and deep neural networks require high levels of computational power; therefore, cost reduction becomes a major concern. Unlearning in federated learning should be highly lightweight and have low latency to be feasible for decentralized resources with a small number of devices. In this context, the amount of memory used, the amount of power consumed, and the time taken by CPUs and GPUs follow, which researchers use to measure computational overhead. These factors are particularly critical to cloud-based solutions, where economic and environmental sustainability are the core issues.

Finally, scalability is used to determine how an unlearning technique is able to sustain performance as the model size or data volume increases. Good unlearning methods should be gracefully scalable, allowing large models to support large or repeated removal requests without incurring massive performance losses. Other methods have been used to improve scalability (such as model pruning) and allowable gradient updates, making machine unlearning more viable in practice.

4.4 MODEL UTILITY

Once the process of unlearning has been implemented, ensuring that the new model will remain efficient becomes necessary. Another key issue in machine unlearning is maintaining model utility, that is, the ability of the model to provide correct and reliable predictions on previously unseen data without considering intentionally deleted data. In previous studies [14, 23, 24], it is important to note that in the course of unlearning, the performance of a model should not change significantly after the event. As unlearning of training data may cause a decrease in predictive performance, measuring the post-unlearning ability is important to ensure that the model can continue to be used and relied upon.

The first is accuracy retention, which is an important measure of model utility and indicates how much the initial predictive performance of the model is retained after unlearning. The unlearning process should, in an ideal scenario, affect only the predictions that are directly related to the data that are being forgotten, and the overall performance of the model should be unaffected. An example of this is when a financial forecasting model is not trained to utilize the data within a certain time period and is expected to forecast the future direction using the data within a different time period. Techniques such as selective retraining and incremental learning have been offered to reduce the loss of accuracy. Specifically, selective retraining transfers knowledge on the basis of the retained model, which is retained only by updating the components of the model that have been influenced by the deleted data.

"Robustness" is a term used to denote the stability and reliability of a model after unlearning. When a model becomes hypersensitive or unstable upon deleting data, its generalizability is undermined. Adversarial testing is a common method for evaluating robustness, where the model is applied to slightly perturbed inputs, and whether the model can be applied consistently is checked. A strongly unlearned model must still be reliable when there is variation in the input.

Another vital aspect of fairness is post-unlearning model utility. Deleting data can lead to the creation of biases or an increase in the number of biases, especially in sensitive tasks such as hiring, loaning, or credit ratings. For example, when a recruitment model is not trained on data concerning a given group of people, it should not be biased toward that group. Equity-conscious unlearning methods are designed to ensure that unlearning does not adversely affect equitable decision-making, which is not only unethical but also legally obligatory in several real-life contexts.

Machine learning models are being continuously updated because new data are available. The consistency between updates reflects the degree to which a model can absorb new data following unlearning without suddenly and unexpectedly developing undesirable behaviors. The unlearning of some of the users' preferences should not affect the performance of the recommender system in terms of its capacity to make relevant suggestions to other users. A consistent model has the same behavior in subsequent updates and unlearnings and therefore has long-term reliability.

4.5 MACHINE UNLEARNING TOOLS AND FRAMEWORKS

Designing efficient machine unlearning algorithms has to meet a number of basic requirements.

4.5.1 Design Requirements

4.5.1.1 Verifiability

In addition to making unlearning requests, users can frequently demand that their information be deleted and that their privacy be preserved. As a result, an effective unlearning model must offer systems for confirming effective unlearning. Backdoor attacks, during which certain triggers are added to the training data, are proposed as one of the proposed solutions [25]. If these triggers can be identified in the original model but not in the unlearned model, then the unlearning process is said to have been successful. These techniques, however, can be obtrusive and can be subject to false positives since backdoor detection is always uncertain, to the detriment of placing legal reliance on them.

4.5.1.2 Consistency

A good unlearning algorithm must be consistent [14]; that is, a model obtained through unlearning must predict the same data as that obtained by retraining an initial model on the retained data. The consistency may be measured by determining the percentage of the same prediction by the two models on a test set. This criterion may also be included as one of the optimization goals in the unlearning process.

4.5.1.3 Accuracy

When a model is unlearned, it must be predictively accurate as well as a retrained model. Because full retraining is usually computationally infeasible, accuracy is usually evaluated on a new test set or against the performance of the original model [26]. An acceptable level of accuracy is necessary to guarantee the practical usability of the unlearned model.

4.5.2 Validation of Machine Unlearning

Unlearning validation is aimed at guaranteeing that an unlearned model cannot be distinguished from a retrained model trained without forgotten data [27]. This is an especially difficult task since cloud service providers might purport the deletion of some data, as other leftover information is still left in the model [26]. The loss of a few samples in large and complicated models may have a minimal effect on the overall performance. Additionally, other users may offer such similar data, which would allow the model to make correct predictions even when certain samples are deleted, which would complicate the validation even more. The simplest validation technique is to retrain the model without the lost samples and compare the model to the untrained model.

4.5.2.1 Membership Inference Attack

Membership inference attacks seek to identify whether model information is spilled over to its training data [28, 29]. Within this framework, an attacker uses the training sample to create an inference model to determine whether a sample belongs to the training sample or not. A collection of shadow models is usually trained on data distributions that are analogous to the target model [30]. The predictions of these shadow models are then learned by the attack model to determine the membership status. These attacks are efficient at identifying the leakage of data; thus, they are useful in authenticating machine unlearning [28].

4.5.2.2 Backdoor Attacks

Backdoor attacks are associated with the insertion of bad triggers into training data to bend the behavior of a model [31]. A backdoored model works normally on clean data, but when a certain trigger is introduced, the prediction is inaccurate. Backdoor attacks were used in [32] to validate the effectiveness of machine unlearning; specifically, all users trained the model with a mixture of clean and toxic data, and some users wanted their data to be deleted. Whereas the rate of false validation can be decreased by increasing the percentage of toxic samples, this measure does not guarantee that the samples are correct. Moreover, the backdoor triggers should not be identified by cloud servers. To overcome this problem, a set of invisible backdoor triggers has been suggested, which can be used to authenticate unlearn and ensure that dishonest servers do not produce validation proofs [33].

4.5.3 Metrics

Many metrics have been suggested for assessing machine unlearning techniques. The lack of an integrated assessment system is due to the multiplicity of goals and methodological beliefs in the various approaches. The evaluation methods can be broadly divided into evaluation metrics and verification methods. Evaluation metrics are used to measure unlearning effectiveness, whereas verification methods are used to determine whether the unlearned models can be distinguished from the retrained models. The typical evaluation metrics are the accuracy of the forget and retain sets, the error rate, the relearn time, the Anamnesis Index, and a number of measures based on distance. The techniques of verification usually depend on attacks or measures of unlearning cost.

4.5.3.1 Accuracy on the Forget Set

Accuracy measures the proportion of correctly classified instances out of the total instances in a dataset [34]. It is calculated as the number of correct predictions divided by the total number of predictions, often expressed as a percentage. In machine unlearning techniques, the accuracy is measured on the forget set Du and refers to the model's performance on the subset of data designated for unlearning. The accuracy of Du is close to that of the retrained model. Ideally, this accuracy should be low [35].

4.5.3.2 Retain Set Accuracy

The accuracy on the retain set Dr refers to the model's performance on the data subset that remains unchanged after unlearning. The goal of the accuracy of Dr is to closely match the performance of the original model before unlearning. This metric assesses how well the model retains its classification ability on the data it was initially trained on but without the forget set [35].

4.5.3.3 Error Rate

The error rate is calculated as (1 – accuracy) on the retained set. It measures the proportion of misclassified instances in the data subset that remains unchanged after unlearning [36].

4.5.3.4 Relearn Time

Relearn time is used to measure the amount of time that a model still remembers about the information that has been marked as being unlearned. It is used to determine the speed with which the model can regain its predictive capacity on the forgotten data when retraining is performed. When an untrained model achieves a performance level similar to that of the original source model, within just a few retraining epochs, it is an indication of residual traces: that the unlearned data are embedded in the model parameters and thus are not fully unlearned [37].

4.5.3.5 Anamnesis Index

The Anamnesis Index is a higher-order measure of relearning behavior because the relearn time of an unlearned model is compared to the relearn time of a model that was trained starting with only the retained data. It normalizes the relearn time by considering a margin of $\alpha\%$ around the model's original accuracy before unlearning. The Anamnesis Index is an indicator of the resistance of the forgotten knowledge as well as the effectiveness of the entire process of unlearning by jointly explaining the relearning speed and the level of baseline performance [35].

4.5.3.6 Distance

Approximate unlearning techniques can also be tested by assessing the distance between the parameters or behavior of the unlearned model and a trained model that is fully retrained. A small distance means that there is a high probability that the two models will make similar predictions, which implies successful unlearning [38].

- **Activation distance:** Activation-based metrics provide a fairly weak yet computationally convenient type of evaluation. The L1 distance between the unlearned model final-layer activations and the retrained model final-layer activations is calculated via this method. The lower values of the L1-norms suggest a better fit between the two models and, by default, more effective unlearning [39]
- **Weight distance:** As the majority of approximate unlearning methods work by adjusting model parameters, weight-based similarity measures are typically employed. The distance between the weights of the unlearned and retrained models is measured via metrics such as the L2-norm distance and cosine similarity, with lower distances or greater similarity implying that the unlearned model has performed better in unlearning. Nevertheless, these measures can be quite difficult to train and can be influenced by errors

in numerical precision. To address these shortcomings, Thudi et al. [40] suggested an extended L2-norm measure that compared the final unlearned weights and the initial model weights and hence avoided naive retraining, leading to minimization of the computational overhead.

- **Distribution distance:** The output distribution between unlearned and retrained models provides more powerful assurance of unlearning efficacy but is more complicated to compute. It is usually used to estimate the Kullback–Leibler (KL) divergence, where the closer to zero this value is the more similar the two datasets are. Chundawat et al. [41] proposed the zero-retrain forgetting measure, which is founded on Jensen–Sharon divergence, and the measure of the distributions of outputs from before and after unlearning.

4.5.3.7 Attacks

Attack-based metrics assess the effectiveness of unlearning in evaluating the privacy and integrity attack resistance of a model, including membership inference and backdoor attacks. During such tests, adversarial examples are made to observe whether unlearned models can effectively remedy efforts to deduce training membership or to make use of a backdoor concealed within them.

4.5.3.8 Unlearning Cost (Storage and Time Cost)

Unlearning cost is a measure of the resources needed to implement the unlearning process, with the storage and computational time taken into consideration. The storage cost is composed of the memory required to store the original model parameters, intermediate states, and other auxiliary information that may be needed during the process of unlearning. The time cost is used to show the duration of the unlearning process, which can use iterative updates to delete or modify learned representations. Efficient unlearning techniques strive to reduce storage and time waste without compromising efficiency.

4.5.3.9 Certified Unlearning

Certified unlearning, initially introduced by Guo et al. [42], provides formal guarantees with noise added to model weights or loss functions, according to the principle of differential privacy. This strategy guarantees that the results of an untrained model are statistically similar to those of a retrained model. These methods of certification are usually applicable only to models whose loss functions are convex and cannot be applied directly to nonconvex optimization landscapes associated with deep learning models.

4.5.3.10 Invasive Metric

Unlearning is checked by invasive metrics, which is an active two-step watermarking and verification procedure [42]. In the watermarking step, the data contributors add recognizable marks to the data or model parameters, which can later be utilized to detect deletions. During the verification phase, the contributors examine the unlearning result as soon as the service provider states completion. This process should be carried out secretly, without the knowledge of the model provider; otherwise, the model provider will attempt to deliberately manipulate the verification results.

- **Watermark-based metric:** Watermarking embeds backdoor triggers or owner-specific binary strings into the data (e.g., $\mathcal{D}$u, model parameters) and creates adversarial examples to capture the unique properties of the model to assist unlearning verification [42].
- **Backdoor-based watermark:** Sommer et al. [43] conducted a verification through a backdoor. The process begins with the watermarking step, in which data contributors design backdoor patterns that change the predictions of $\mathcal{D}$u to an artificial target label. The poisoned samples (watermarks) are then uploaded to the server. During the verification step, once the model has completed unlearning, data contributors evaluate the statistics on the backdoor success rate. If the model retains the relevant information of $\mathcal{D}$u, the backdoor success rate will be notably high.
- **Feature-based watermark:** Izzo et al. [44] proposed the feature injection test, which is used mainly for the unlearning verification of linear classifiers. The watermarking step injects a strong signal into $\mathcal{D}$u, involving the addition of an extra feature that is set to zero. The training process assigns a significantly different weight from zero to this feature. The verification step is as follows: because unlearning causes the weight of this feature to become zero again, unlearning can be verified by detecting the change in the unlearned model's weight for this special feature before and after deletion. The closer the change is to zero, the more successful the unlearning is.
- **Adversarial example-based watermark:** The advancement of adversarial watermarking in federated learning was suggested by Gao et al. [42]. Since the unique nature of a deep neural network classifier can be represented by its classification boundary [45], they leveraged boundary fingerprinting [45] to find decision boundary fingerprints as watermarks for uniquely identifying the local model. Specifically, starting with a watermarking step, data contributors produce adversarial examples as watermarks near the decision boundary to characterize the robustness of the local model. The local model is then fine-tuned to obtain a watermarked local model that demonstrates a smoother (robust) boundary around the watermarks. The watermarked local model is then transmitted to the server for aggregation into the global model. The final step is verification, which checks the prediction results of the global model on adversarial watermarks. Given that genuine unlearning is expected to rapidly diminish the smoothed (robust) boundary around the watermarks, incorrect model predictions indicate successful unlearning.

4.5.3.11 Noninvasive Metric

In most real-world applications, the contributors of data may not have implanted watermarks in the data beforehand to authenticate the claim of unlearning by model providers, as is common with legacy models. In addition, invasive verification methods also have the potential to cause security risks, and the efficiency of such methods can be compromised by defensive measures by model providers. In this case, noninvasive measures provide an acceptable variant. These methods are based on observable model outputs, or the model provider may have to provide cryptographic evidence, thus allowing verification of unlearning without altering the data or the model during training.

4.5.3.12 Membership Inference Metric

Membership inference algorithms estimate whether a particular data sample is used in the training of a model [46], so they are very appropriate for determining whether residual information is present. In their unlearning verification, Graves et al. [23] trained a shadow model that mimics the behavior of the unlearned model, after which membership inference was used to verify the unlearned model. They first trained a shadow model to mimic the unlearned model and then trained a binary meta-classifier with the shadow model's output (e.g., predictive probability or confidence) on both training and nontraining data as metadata. Finally, this metaclassifier determines whether $\mathcal{D}u$ is still in the training dataset via a similar format of metadata from the unlearned model. As a continuation of this concept, Liu et al. [47] introduced the forgetting rate (FR), which quantifies a change in the membership inference accuracy, pre-unlearning versus post-unlearning. The FR offers an intuitive measure of the success rate of member inference on $\mathcal{D}u$, which changes from member to nonmember after unlearning. When the FR value is 1, $\mathcal{D}u$ has completely changed from a member to a nonmember, and unlearning is successful.

4.5.3.13 Data Reconstruction Metric

The goal of data reconstruction attacks is to estimate information about the training data of a model through manipulation of either model outputs in black-box scenarios or model parameters in white-box scenarios [46]. In [46], unlearning was carried out at the class level and not at the individual sample level. The authors modified a threat model that was initially presented in [48] to reconstruct the information of a particular class to confirm the elimination of a complete class. The reconstruction process commences with the initialization of the input vector to a set of zeros and the addition of minor noise. Gradient descent optimization of the threat model is then performed with respect to the target (forgotten) class via a loss function. The image processing steps are periodically performed to aid interpretation of the generated samples. This process is repeated several times in the epochs to obtain the final reconstructed images. When unlearning is performed correctly, the reconstructed outputs of the unlearned model do not have any recognizable information that is related to the forgotten class.

4.5.3.14 Cryptographic-Based Metric

Since many current unlearning verification techniques do not have explicit theoretical guarantees, Eisenhofer et al. [49] presented the first protocol in this regard, which involves verifiable unlearning with cryptographic guarantees. Their framework uses short noninteractive arguments of knowledge to perform verifiable computations to show that updates to models driven by unlearning have been performed correctly. Additionally, the hash chains are utilized to represent the nonmembership of particular data samples in the training set. This protocol, which is used by model providers, can provide cryptographic evidence that an agreed-upon unlearning procedure has been subsequently executed to provide powerful and principled verification assurances.

4.6 UNLEARNING VERIFICATION

Unlearning verification methods aim to attest to the fact that an unlearned model cannot be easily differentiated from a model retrained with fresh data without the deleted data. Although unlearning metrics are mainly used as theoretical guidelines to direct and optimize machine unlearning processes, unlearning verification techniques are used in a post hoc manner and are post hoc certificates that confirm the successful attainment of unlearning. The approaches also offer the best practice in the efficient evaluation of the accuracy of unlearned models.

Notably, unlearning metrics and verification metrics can be similar in one aspect; however, their essence is different. Unlearning metrics can either be part of optimization goals or be applied to provide constrained guarantees, but verification metrics are available to provide evaluation and validation only.

4.6.1 Feature Injection Test

The feature injection test aims at confirming that an untuned model has efficiently modified the parameters that are linked to the deleted data samples utilizing data features or attributes [44]. The rationale behind this is that when the data intended to be dropped have a very distinct characteristic that they share with the rest of the data, it will have a robust effect on the parameters that are being learned by the model. To be effective, however, the injected feature should also be associated with the labels of the data to be forgotten; otherwise, the model may be unable to learn any meaningful associations.

To be more exact, an extra feature is added to each data sample to ensure that it assumes a value of zero to the retained dataset and is perfectly correlated with labels of the data to forget. This method was demonstrated by Izzo et al. [44], who used linear classifiers, where the parameter that corresponds to the feature injected should be significantly different than zero after training. This parameter is supposed to return to zero after unlearning. As a result, the difference in the weights before and after unlearning can be visualized and employed as a quantitative measure of the effectiveness of the unlearning process.

One of the main weaknesses of this method of verification is that at the moment, it is applicable only to linear and logistic models [44]. This limitation is related to the fact that these types of models make direct correlations between parameters and specific features, and it is not easy to generalize this technique to more complicated models, including deep neural networks, even in cases where the data to be forgotten are sparse. Another weakness is that a modified dataset containing injected features must be prepared beforehand, and the model must be trained either in advance or in an incremental fashion depending on what learning paradigm the user is using.

4.6.2 Forgetting Measuring

Although purportedly deleted data samples have been removed from a model, traces of such data samples may still be present [50]. Jagielski et al. [50] developed a formal model for quantifying the extent of forgetfulness of a model that is based on privacy-based attacks. In particular, a model is α-forgettable for a training sample when a privacy attack, such as a membership inference attack, has at least an α success rate applied to the sample. This concept of forgetfulness is looser than that of differential privacy, which demands that a training algorithm forget each sample that it processes on the fly. Conversely, the α-forgetting definition enables the learning of a sample momentarily and is concerned with quantifying the time or extent of reduction in the effects of a sample in the model.

4.6.3 Information Leakage

Most machine learning models involve data that leak in nature when the model is updated [51]. This characteristic has been used recently to compare the state of a model before and after unlearning to estimate the amount of information leakage. Specifically, Salem et al. [52] proposed an adversarial attack in the image space that can reconstruct a sample that has been deleted from a classifier following unlearning. Chen et al. [51] developed a membership inference attack to establish whether a dropped sample belongs to the original training set. In contrast to the previous methods [52], their method also utilizes the posterior output distributions of both the original and the unlearned models. Moreover, to describe information leakage, Chen et al. [51] developed two quantitative measures, namely, the degradation count and the degradation rate. The degradation count is the ratio between the target samples where membership can be determined with greater confidence by the proposed attack than by traditional attacks and the overall number of samples. The degradation rate is the mean increase in the level of confidence of the suggested attack compared with traditional attacks.

4.6.4 Membership Inference Attacks

This type of attack is designed to detect whether a target model leaks data. Specifically, an inference model is trained to recognize new data samples from the training data used to optimize the target model. In [53], a set of shallow models was trained on a new set of data items different from the one on which the target model was trained. The attack model was then trained to predict whether a data item belonged to the training data on the basis of the predictions made by shallow models for training as well as testing data. The training sets for the shallow and attack models have similar data distributions to those of the target model. Membership inference attacks are helpful for detecting data leaks. Hence, they are useful for verifying the effectiveness of machine unlearning [51].

4.6.5 Backdoor Attacks

Backdoor attacks have the original purpose of introducing malicious triggers to training data to mislead machine learning models [54]. A compromised model acts correctly on clean inputs; when introduced to poisoned inputs with a particular trigger of a target class, it makes incorrect predictions. Backdoor attacks are exploited in [43] as one of the procedures for checking the performance of machine unlearning. Within this context, a model is first trained on a set of data of a combination of clean and poisoned samples provided by various users. After that, a group of users demands that their information be deleted. When the unlearning process is not able to remove all the requested data, the poisoned samples still activate the backdoor and are categorized under the target class. However, if unlearning succeeds, the model will no longer associate the trigger with the target class and will therefore be unable to misclassify the poisoned samples. However, this criterion is not a guarantee of absolute correctness. It is not possible to obtain a probability of false conclusions of zero, but it can decrease with the increasing number of poisoned samples.

4.6.6 Slow-Down Attacks

A number of machine unlearning studies focus on conceptual assurances of the inability to differentiate between unlearned models and scratch-trained models. Nevertheless, such works are usually not guided by practical limitations in terms of computational cost and efficiency [55]. As a result, a new threat has been introduced to machine unlearning, where poisoning attacks are used to slow down the unlearning process.

4.6.7 Interclass Confusion Test

The interclass confusion test aims at testing the possibility of inferring information contained in the data to be removed into an unlearned model [56]. In contrast to the traditional approximate definition of unlearning, which determines the indistinguishability between the unlearned and retrained models in the parameter space, the test is used to measure the unlearning performance of the model in the output space by examining the prediction behavior of the model on different classes.

4.6.8 Federated Verification

Verifying unlearning in federated learning is a unique challenge. First, the entry or exit of a single or few clients may cause slight changes in the performance of the global model, making it difficult to verify the model on the basis of the output. Second, adversarial attack-based verification methods do not usually fit the federated setting and can add extra security risks to the underlying infrastructure [57].

To resolve these issues, Gao et al. [57] suggested a verification mechanism based on a few communication rounds, which allows the clients to check for the existence or nonexistence of their information in the global model. This method is highly consistent with the paradigms of federated learning since it adheres to the same pattern of iterative communication between customers and the central server during normal federated training.

4.6.9 Cryptographic Proofs

Since the majority of the current unlearning verification schemes do not provide formal theoretical guarantees, Eisenhofer et al. [58] proposed a cryptography-informed protocol to compute two proofs, that is, a proof of update (the model was trained on a particular dataset *D*) and a proof of unlearning (the forget item *d* is not a member of *D*). The demonstration of updates is based on a SNARK-based data structure [59] to capture cryptographic commitments as hashes every time the model is subjected to learning or unlearning. This process is such that (1) the model is fitted only to the rest of the data, (2) the remaining current data do not contain any items that are marked as being forgotten, (3) the previously defined forget set is a subset of the current forget set, and (4) the forgotten items are never reintroduced into the training data. The core idea of the proof of unlearning is to use the Merkle tree to maintain the order of the data items in the training data so that an unlearned item cannot be added to the training data again. While the approach is demonstrated on efficient retraining (SISA) [60], it is applicable for any unlearning method.

REFERENCES

1. Joshi, A., Saha, S., Shukla, D., Vema, S., Jhamtani, H., Gaur, M., & Modi, A. (2024). Toward robust evaluation of unlearning in llms via data transformations. *arXiv preprint arXiv:2411.15477.*
2. Maini, P., Feng, Z., Schwarzschild, A., Lipton, Z. C., & Kolter, J. Z. (2024). Tofu: A task of fictitious unlearning for llms. *arXiv preprint arXiv:2401.06121.*
3. https://www.wmdp.ai/
4. Li, N., Pan, A., Gopal, A., Yue, S., Berrios, D., Gatti, A., . . . & Hendrycks, D. (2024). The WMDP benchmark: Measuring and reducing malicious use with unlearning. *arXiv preprint arXiv:2403.03218.*
5. https://www.kaggle.com/c/cifar-10
6. https://www.kaggle.com/datasets/hojjatk/mnist-dataset
7. https://www.kaggle.com/datasets/zalando-research/fashionmnist
8. Jahin, M. A., Mridha, M. F., Dey, N., & Hossen, M. J. (2026). Human-in-the-loop feature selection using interpretable Kolmogorov-Arnold network-based double deep Q-network. IEEE Open Journal of the Computer Society, 7, 389–403. https://doi.org/10.1109/OJCS.2026.3652986
9. Jahin, M. A., Masud, M. A., Suva, M. W., Mridha, M. F., & Dey, N. (2025). Lorentz-equivariant quantum graph neural network for high-energy physics. IEEE Transactions on Artificial Intelligence, 6(12), 3195–3206. https://doi.org/10.1109/TAI.2025.3554461
10. https://susanqq.github.io/UTKFace/
11. https://github.com/ndb796/MachineUnlearning
12. Shi, W., Lee, J., Huang, Y., Malladi, S., Zhao, J., Holtzman, A., . . . & Zhang, C. (2024). Muse: Machine unlearning six-way evaluation for language models. *arXiv preprint arXiv:2407.06460.*
13. Thaker, P., Hu, S., Kale, N., Maurya, Y., Wu, Z. S., & Smith, V. (2025, April). Position: Llm unlearning benchmarks are weak measures of progress. In 2025 IEEE Conference on Secure and Trustworthy Machine Learning (SaTML) (pp. 520–533). IEEE.
14. Cao, Y., & Yang, J. (2015, May). Toward making systems forget with machine unlearning. In 2015 IEEE Symposium on Security and Privacy (pp. 463–480). IEEE.

15. Izzo, Z., Smart, M. A., Chaudhuri, K., & Zou, J. (2021, March). Approximate data deletion from machine learning models. In International Conference on Artificial Intelligence and Statistics (pp. 2008–2016). PMLR.
16. Guo, C., Goldstein, T., Hannun, A., & Van Der Maaten, L. (2019). Certified data removal from machine learning models. *arXiv preprint arXiv:1911.03030.*
17. Wu, Y., Dobriban, E., & Davidson, S. (2020, November). Deltagrad: Rapid retraining of machine learning models. In International Conference on Machine Learning (pp. 10355–10366). PMLR.
18. Brophy, J., & Lowd, D. (2021, July). Machine unlearning for random forests. In International Conference on Machine Learning (pp. 1092–1104). PMLR.
19. Chundawat, V. S., Tarun, A. K., Mandal, M., & Kankanhalli, M. (2023). Zero-shot machine unlearning. IEEE Transactions on Information Forensics and Security, 18, 2345–2354.
20. Golatkar, A., Achille, A., Ravichandran, A., Polito, M., & Soatto, S. (2021). Mixed-privacy forgetting in deep networks. In Proceedings of the IEEE/CVF Conference on Computer Vision and Pattern Recognition (pp. 792–801).
21. Tarun, A. K., Chundawat, V. S., Mandal, M., & Kankanhalli, M. (2023). Fast yet effective machine unlearning. IEEE Transactions on Neural Networks and Learning Systems, 35(9), 13046–13055.
22. Ginart, A., Guan, M., Valiant, G., & Zou, J. Y. (2019). Making AI forget you: Data deletion in machine learning. Advances in Neural Information Processing Systems, 32.
23. Graves, L., Nagisetty, V., & Ganesh, V. (2021, May). Amnesiac machine learning. In Proceedings of the AAAI Conference on Artificial Intelligence (Vol. 35, No. 13, pp. 11516–11524).
24. Sekhari, A., Acharya, J., Kamath, G., & Suresh, A. T. (2021). Remember what you want to forget: Algorithms for machine unlearning. Advances in Neural Information Processing Systems, 34, 18075–18086.
25. Li, C., Jiang, H., Chen, J., Zhao, Y., Fu, S., Jing, F., & Guo, Y. (2025). An overview of machine unlearning. High-Confidence Computing, 5(2), 100254.
26. He, Y., Meng, G., Chen, K., He, J., & Hu, X. (2021). Deepobliviate: A powerful charm for erasing data residual memory in deep neural networks. *arXiv preprint arXiv:2105.06209.*
27. Thudi, A., Jia, H., Shumailov, I., & Papernot, N. (2022). On the necessity of auditable algorithmic definitions for machine unlearning. In 31st USENIX Security Symposium (USENIX Security 22) (pp. 4007–4022).
28. Chen, M., Zhang, Z., Wang, T., Backes, M., Humbert, M., & Zhang, Y. (2021, November). When machine unlearning jeopardizes privacy. In Proceedings of the 2021 ACM SIGSAC Conference on Computer and Communications Security (pp. 896–911).
29. Thudi, A., Shumailov, I., Boenisch, F., & Papernot, N. (2022). Bounding membership inference. *arXiv preprint arXiv:2202.12232.*
30. Shokri, R., Stronati, M., Song, C., & Shmatikov, V. (2017, May). Membership inference attacks against machine learning models. In 2017 IEEE Symposium on Security and Privacy (SP) (pp. 3–18). IEEE.
31. Wang, B., Yao, Y., Shan, S., Li, H., Viswanath, B., Zheng, H., & Zhao, B. Y. (2019, May). Neural cleanse: Identifying and mitigating backdoor attacks in neural networks. In 2019 IEEE Symposium on Security and Privacy (SP) (pp. 707–723). IEEE.
32. Sommer, D. M., Song, L., Wagh, S., & Mittal, P. (2022). Athena: Probabilistic verification of machine unlearning. Proceedings on Privacy Enhancing Technologies.
33. Guo, Y., Zhao, Y., Hou, S., Wang, C., & Jia, X. (2023). Verifying in the dark: Verifiable machine unlearning by using invisible backdoor triggers. IEEE Transactions on Information Forensics and Security, 19, 708–721.

34. Wu, G., Hashemi, M., & Srinivasa, C. (2022). PUMA: Performance unchanged model augmentation for training data removal. *arXiv 2022, arXiv:2203.00846.*
35. Chundawat, V. S., Tarun, A. K., Mandal, M., & Kankanhalli, M. (2023). Zero-shot machine unlearning. IEEE Transactions Information Forensics and Security, 18, 2345–2354.
36. Koch, K., & Soll, M. (2023, February 8–10). No matter how you slice it: Machine unlearning with SISA comes at the expense of minority classes. In Proceedings of the 2023 IEEE Conference on Secure and Trustworthy Machine Learning (SaTML), Raleigh, NC, USA.
37. Tarun, A. K., Chundawat, V. S., Mandal, M., & Kankanhalli, M. (2024). Fast however, effective machine unlearning. IEEE Transactions on Neural Networks and Learning Systems, 35, 13046–13055.
38. Izzo, Z., Smart, M. A., Chaudhuri, K., & Zou, J. (2021). Approximate data deletion from machine learning models. *arXiv 2021, arXiv:2002.10077.*
39. Golatkar, A., Achille, A., & Soatto, S. (2020). Eternal sunshine of the spotless net: Selective forgetting in deep networks. In Proceedings of the IEEE/CVF Conference on Computer Vision and Pattern Recognition (pp. 9304–9312).
40. Thudi, A., Deza, G., Chandrasekaran, V., & Papernot, N. (2022, June). Unrolling SGD: Understanding factors influencing machine unlearning. In 2022 IEEE 7th European Symposium on Security and Privacy (EuroS&P) (pp. 303–319). IEEE.
41. Chundawat, V. S., Tarun, A. K., Mandal, M., & Kankanhalli, M. (2023, June). Can bad teaching induce forgetting? unlearning in deep networks using an incompetent teacher. In Proceedings of the AAAI Conference on Artificial Intelligence (Vol. 37, No. 6, pp. 7210–7217).
42. Gao, X., Ma, X., Wang, J., Sun, Y., Li, B., Ji, S., . . . & Chen, J. (2024). Verifi: Toward verifiable federated unlearning. IEEE Transactions on Dependable and Secure Computing, 21(6), 5720–5736.
43. Sommer, D. M., Song, L., Wagh, S., & Mittal, P. (2020). Toward probabilistic verification of machine unlearning. *arXiv preprint arXiv:2003.04247.*
44. Izzo, Z., Ying, L., & Zou, J. (2021, July). How to learn when data reacts to your model: Performative gradient descent. In International Conference on Machine Learning (pp. 4641–4650). PMLR.
45. Cao, Y., Yu, A. F., Aday, A., Stahl, E., Merwine, J., & Yang, J. (2018, May). Efficient repair of polluted machine learning systems via causal unlearning. In Proceedings of the 2018 on Asia Conference on Computer and Communications Security (pp. 735–747).
46. Kurmanji, M., Triantafillou, P., & Triantafillou, E. (2023). Toward unbounded machine unlearning. CoRR abs/2302.09880. https://doi.org/10.48550/ARXIV.2302.09880 arXiv: 2302.09880
47. Ma, Z., Liu, Y., Liu, X., Liu, J., Ma, J., & Ren, K. (2022). Learn to forget: Machine unlearning via neuron masking. IEEE Transactions on Dependable and Secure Computing, 20(4), 3194–3207.
48. Fredrikson, M., Jha, S., & Ristenpart, T. (2015, October). Model inversion attacks that exploit confidence information and basic countermeasures. In Proceedings of the 22nd ACM SIGSAC Conference on Computer and Communications Security (pp. 1322–1333).
49. Eisenhofer, T., Riepel, D., Chandrasekaran, V., Ghosh, E., Ohrimenko, O., & Papernot, N. (2025, April). Verifiable and provably secure machine unlearning. In 2025 IEEE Conference on Secure and Trustworthy Machine Learning (SaTML) (pp. 479–496). IEEE.
50. Jagielski, M., Thakkar, O., Tramer, F., Ippolito, D., Lee, K., Carlini, N., . . . & Zhang, C. (2022). Measuring forgetting of memorized training examples. *arXiv preprint arXiv:2207.00099.*

51. Chen, M., Zhang, Z., Wang, T., Backes, M., Humbert, M., & Zhang, Y. (2021, November). When machine unlearning jeopardizes privacy. In Proceedings of the 2021 ACM SIGSAC Conference on Computer and Communications Security (pp. 896–911).
52. Salem, A., Bhattacharya, A., Backes, M., Fritz, M., & Zhang, Y. (2020). {Updates-Leak}: Dataset inference and reconstruction attacks in online learning. In 29th USENIX Security Symposium (USENIX Security 20) (pp. 1291–1308).
53. Shokri, R., Stronati, M., Song, C., & Shmatikov, V. (2017, May). Membership inference attacks against machine learning models. In 2017 IEEE Symposium on Security and Privacy (SP) (pp. 3–18). IEEE.
54. Wang, B., Yao, Y., Shan, S., Li, H., Viswanath, B., Zheng, H., & Zhao, B. Y. (2019, May). Neural cleanse: Identifying and mitigating backdoor attacks in neural networks. In 2019 IEEE Symposium on Security and Privacy (SP) (pp. 707–723). IEEE.
55. Marchant, N. G., Rubinstein, B. I., & Alfeld, S. (2022, June). Hard to forget: Poisoning attacks on certified machine unlearning. In Proceedings of the AAAI Conference on Artificial Intelligence (Vol. 36, No. 7, pp. 7691–7700).
56. Goel, S., Prabhu, A., Sanyal, A., Lim, S. N., Torr, P., & Kumaraguru, P. (2022). Toward adversarial evaluations for inexact machine unlearning. *arXiv preprint arXiv:2201.06640.*
57. Gao, X., Ma, X., Wang, J., Sun, Y., Li, B., Ji, S., . . . & Chen, J. (2024). Verifi: Toward verifiable federated unlearning. IEEE Transactions on Dependable and Secure Computing, 21(6), 5720–5736.
58. Eisenhofer, T., Riepel, D., Chandrasekaran, V., Ghosh, E., Ohrimenko, O., & Papernot, N. (2025, April). Verifiable and provably secure machine unlearning. In 2025 IEEE Conference on Secure and Trustworthy Machine Learning (SaTML) (pp. 479–496). IEEE.
59. Bitansky, N., Canetti, R., Chiesa, A., & Tromer, E. (2012, January). From extractable collision resistance to succinct noninteractive arguments of knowledge, and back again. In Proceedings of the 3rd Innovations in Theoretical Computer Science Conference (pp. 326–349).
60. Bourtoule, L., Chandrasekaran, V., Choquette-Choo, C. A., Jia, H., Travers, A., Zhang, B., . . . & Papernot, N. (2021, May). Machine unlearning. In 2021 IEEE Symposium on Security and Privacy (SP) (pp. 141–159). IEEE.

5 Case Studies in Machine Unlearning

5.1 UNLEARNING IN HEALTHCARE

Currently, several machine learning algorithms have been developed as potent tools to use large volumes of medical data to increase the patient outcomes of diagnostic instruments for therapy recommendations. The responsiveness and adaptability of healthcare managers or organizations to change are crucial to their success in the present healthcare landscape. Change involves learning novel behaviors and the abandonment or relinquishment of some previously existing behaviors—more formally, unlearning [1]. Privacy is a major issue in healthcare settings because of the sensitivity of patient information. Since the adoption of data-driven technologies in healthcare continues to grow, the issues of data privacy and security are becoming even more critical.

Owing to the rapid transformation of healthcare delivery, medical professionals must change their practice behaviors to ensure competence over time [2]. Owing to these changes and the changing evidence base, best-practice recommendations that can inform the practice behaviors of clinicians also differ. To follow these suggestions and deliver modern care to patients, clinicians must first delearn old behavioral patterns before they can be replaced by new skills and techniques that are more evidence based [3, 4].

The selective forgetting of outdated or irrelevant information is incredibly valuable in the sphere of healthcare, where the conditions of a patient, treatment regimens, and medical knowledge constantly change. By removing obsolete data points or outdated treatment paradigms, machine unlearning can ensure that healthcare algorithms are relevant and adaptable to existing healthcare practices and patient demands. Furthermore, machine unlearning is important in the context of privacy and security issues related to healthcare data. It has the ability to selectively delete sensitive or personally identifiable data in datasets, enhancing patient privacy and regulatory compliance [5].

5.1.1 Unlearning versus Deskilling

Since unlearning has been found to be a deliberate process, it should be noted that *unlearning* is not the same as *deskilling*. The distinction between these two processes lies in the degree of intentionality and the outcome of the action [6]. To experience successful unlearning, people must be willing to abandon old and/or destructive habits. The pattern of practice adopted by clinicians can often be habitual, and only conscious effort can break the habit and eliminate the knowledge that is superfluous. Conversely, deskilling is an unintentional phenomenon that is defined as the loss or

DOI: 10.1201/9781003771470-5

forgetting of a skill with time, which is essentially the philosophy of using it or losing it [7]. Another method of differentiating between unlearning and deskilling is the outcome of the action. Unlearning is a process of substituting poor practices with an effective skill, procedure, or technique, in contrast to deskilling, which causes the skill to be lost or forgotten.

Recently, unlearning methods have been considered in the digital healthcare environment to comply with data privacy regulations, especially with regard to medical imaging (8–11). Nasirigerdeh et al. (9) compared the effectiveness of different unlearning algorithms in the medical imaging field. According to their results, approximate unlearning algorithms work well on experimental retain and forget sets but are not generalizable. Deng et al. (8) presented federated client unlearning (FCU) based on model-contrastive unlearning and frequency-guided memory preservation so that specific client data can be eliminated and the overall model performance is not affected. Additionally, authors [8] show the first collaboration-free federated unlearning system, termed Maverick++, to be used in medical imaging. The findings make Maverick++ a convenient, effective, and privacy-conscious system for executing data deletion requests on federated learning to the medical imaging sphere.

However, it is difficult to see that the forget dataset is being erased because most architectures cannot be explained and the models are random. Moreover, medical information is gathered from a variety of sources and forms, such as images and clinical notes [9, 10]. Therefore, the overlap of all these modalities, which is a commonality, inspires the necessity of having multimodal unlearning methods to address the complexities of multimodal practices.

5.1.2 Technical Challenges

Machine unlearning has some technical issues [11] that are related to digital healthcare. The most noteworthy ones include the following:

1. Unlearning, where retraining is performed only on the retained set, is very efficient but is very costly in terms of computational effort. In the event that a patient asks to forget his or her data, precise unlearning would require considerable computational power, thus resulting in delays in providing diagnostic assistance and higher operational expenses. Moreover, it has been demonstrated that exact unlearning leaks information about minority classes [12], which is catastrophic in the sphere of healthcare.
2. The current unlearning algorithms adversely affect the generalizability of the model, especially in cases where the forget set is large. For example, if a machine learning model is requested to forget the data of some patients, it may fail to perform well with clients who possess similar features (e.g., some age groups or medical conditions), which influences the overall performance and justice of the model.
3. Unlearning can make the reasons behind updating the model ambiguous, and it is difficult for healthcare professionals to determine and rely on the decisions of the model. This inability to be transparent may prevent the adoption process and raise concerns about accountability and patient safety.

4. Machine unlearning algorithms cannot be easily integrated into current clinical workflows logistically and organizationally. An example is an electronic health record (EHR) system that uses AI models to forecast disease outbreaks. To achieve machine unlearning, it is important to coordinate the implementation of this system so that it is possible not to interrupt current analyses or the process of data flow when data are removed. The integration process may overburden available resources, leading to reduced efficiency and performance of the EHR system.

Finally, but not least, inattention to machine unlearning in healthcare data may have far-reaching consequences. Outdated models can result in incorrect diagnoses, inadequate treatment suggestions, or discriminatory results; however, more importantly, they can compromise patient safety and undermine confidence in the healthcare system. Additionally, bodies in various countries have stressed the need for clear and responsible AI systems in the healthcare industry [13]. With the implementation of machine unlearning in data practices, healthcare institutions can ensure that their predictive models are robust, accurate, trustworthy, and ethical.

5.1.3 Limitations of Machine Unlearning in Healthcare

Although machine unlearning has the potential to increase flexibility and responsiveness in healthcare, it is also vulnerable to a variety of challenges that should be addressed before successfully implementation. Machine unlearning algorithms depend on the quality and representativeness of the data. Data bias, incompleteness, and inconsistency are common healthcare problems that introduce errors to updates or can result in patients forgetting important information that might negatively affect their treatment. For example, if the data used to train and later update a model are biased, the predictions and decisions made by the model will be biased, and different groups of patients may be treated unequally [14].

Although it is necessary to unlearn outdated or irrelevant information so that the model can be adapted to the needs of every patient, there is a possibility that one may forget the important knowledge or patterns that he or she might be applying in patient care. Balancing the necessity of becoming more adaptable and the necessity of retaining the required knowledge is complicated. For example, unlearning algorithms eliminate infrequent yet clinically valuable patterns in patient data, which may result in worse clinical outcomes [15].

5.1.4 Unlearning in Digital Healthcare

Digital healthcare unlearning techniques have been applied fairly recently to digital healthcare to comply with the regulations of data privacy, especially in medical imaging [16–19]. Within the medical community, the computerization of medical records, medical diagnosis results, and patient data has led to an era of unparalleled access to massive historical information repositories [20]. Nevertheless, a major challenge exists, in conjunction with this abundance of information, in how to manage and utilize data efficiently [21]. In this case, machine unlearning emerges as an important element in making the most of the use of these digitized healthcare data to allow healthcare systems to refine their data analysis processes by dynamically changing with changing datasets.

Nasirigerdeh et al. [17] determined the performance of different unlearning algorithms in medical imaging. According to their findings, approximate unlearning algorithms are good at retaining and forgetting sets but are not generalizable. Deng et al. [16] proposed FCU, which uses model-contrastive unlearning and frequency-directed memory maintenance to effectively delete certain client data without systematically prevalent performance of the model.

The importance of machine learning in healthcare cannot be denied. With ever-changing medical knowledge and patient demographics, fixed models are likely to become ineffective and patient outcomes may be jeopardized. The solution to this problem is through machine unlearning algorithms, which allow models to update their knowledge base continuously and be useful in dynamic situations. Moreover, through the use of machine unlearning, healthcare organizations can use data-driven information to pursue innovation, enhance patient care, and ultimately save lives. Unlearning in healthcare involves changing the skills of practitioners by unlearning from their previous knowledge. The unlearning process might result in medical errors, as practitioners might fall back to their habits when they are under cognitive pressure, particularly when there are sudden changes in technology and higher information processing needs [22].

5.2 UNLEARNING IN FINANCIAL SERVICES AND DATA RETENTION

Federated unlearning is important in financial services, especially unlearning, to comply with laws and rules and to keep data confidential. By doing so, financial institutions are able to selectively drop data in machine learning models without full retraining, thereby increasing model flexibility and security.

In financial services, federated unlearning has been applied to improve data retention compliance and privacy by allowing institutions to selectively remove certain data points from models [23]. This is enabled by the fact that it ensures that models are correct and adjustable and, less frequently, that expensive retraining is needed to meet regulatory demands. In this respect, Brodzinski [24] addresses the unlearning of machines in financial services and how secure data retention practices are necessary. It emphasizes threats such as membership inference attacks and the importance of strong defenses, such as differential privacy, to ensure the integrity and privacy of sensitive financial data. Conversely, graph unlearning in financial services [25] aims to delete sensitive data through transaction systems while adhering to privacy laws. It covers issues such as accuracy and efficiency of computation and stresses the necessity of effective mechanisms that safeguard user data when saving and deleting.

Machine unlearning in financial services addresses data retention, where models can be requested to forget sensitive information, thereby increasing privacy protection. This process reduces the risks of privacy and security attacks and ensures that the regulations are followed and that the data of customers are maintained [26].

5.3 MACHINE UNLEARNING IN SOCIAL MEDIA AND USER DATA CONTROL

Unlearning through social media machines is a component of user data management and is a significant issue concerning privacy laws, such as the GDPR and CCPA. It allows the elimination of certain data from machine learning models without affecting the overall performance of the models. This process is necessary to maintain the right to be forgotten; thus, everyone can demand that his or her personal information be deleted. The concept of machine unlearning in social media allows users to exercise their right to be forgotten by providing the option of deleting their personal data and affecting the model of machine learning, thereby giving users more control over their data and privacy policy. Researchers [27] cover machine unlearning systems such as SISA and AmnesiacML, which help satisfy the right to be forgotten in social media, allowing the deletion of personal information in trained models and considering the question of fairness in AI ethics. Nonetheless, the methods should address domain-specific biases and adjust to the peculiarities of the data so that unlearning can be efficient; at the same time, users can trust the model and model performance can be preserved [28].

One study [29] proposed a new machine unlearning privacy-preserving mechanism that can be applied to any machine learning model. It uses shadow models as a defense mechanism to defend against deleted data in a white-box case. According to the proposed approach, a machine learning model is created by the linear combination of the unlearned model and shadow models, and it reduces adversarial attacks more than 13% in accuracy.

5.3.1 Challenges and Future Directions

Privacy and security risks: The current level of privacy and security suggests that machine unlearning introduces novel weaknesses, which need to be explored further and addressed with more robust solutions [30].

Taxonomy and evaluation: An extensive taxonomy of unlearning methods and their performance is needed to inform future research and practice in different contexts [31].

Although machine unlearning has a variety of positive effects on the control of user data, ethical and security-related issues are also present, which should be considered at implementation.

5.4 SOCIAL BIAS MITIGATION IN LANGUAGE MODELS VIA MACHINE UNLEARNING

Machine unlearning, as a method of mitigating social bias in language models, is a promising direction for removing existing biases in AI systems. This methodology enables one to selectively forget unpleasant behaviors without undergoing lengthy retraining; therefore, it provides a more effective solution.

5.4.1 Machine Unlearning Techniques

Partitioned contrastive gradient unlearning (PCGU): This approach identifies certain biases in decoder models, which have been proven to lower bias scores with little decrease in performance [32]. The authors apply distributed PCGU to large models, which increases its applicability to state-of-the-art language models.

Negation through task vector: This method outperforms the PCGU and achieves an 11.8% reduction in bias scores on the LLaMA-27B while preserving model performance [32]. This empirically proves that negation via the task vector approach is better at eliminating social biases than the PCGU is and does not harm model performance or perplexity.

Mask language modeling unlearning: This approach aims to reduce the probability of producing biased content, essentially allowing language models to forget damaging associations [33]. This study reveals that the unexpected possibility of cross-domain transfer unlearning exists, meaning that in one type of bias, debiasing can alleviate other forms of bias.

REFERENCES

1. Coombs, C. R., Hislop, D., Holland, J., Bosley, S. L. C., & Manful, E. (2013). Exploring types of individual unlearning by local health-care managers: An original empirical approach. Health and Social Care Delivery Research, 1(2), 1–126.
2. Welch Bacon, C. E., Pike Lacy, A. M., & Lam, K. C. (2021). Knowledge translation in athletic training: Considerations for bridging the knowledge-to-practice gap. Journal of Athletic Train, 56(11), 1165–1172. https://doi.org/10.4085/0470-20
3. Newman, M. B. (2019). Unlearning: Enabling professional success in an ever-changing environment. Professional Case Management, 24(5), 262–264.
4. Khosravy, M., Gupta, N., Dey, N., & Witkowski, O. (2025, February). Are LLMs ready to shoulder biomedical trust? In International Conference on Innovations in Biotechnology and Health Sciences (pp. 125–142). Singapore: Springer Nature Singapore.
5. Alvandi, A. O. (2024, June). Machine unlearning in digitalized healthcare arena a comprehensive exploration. OSF.
6. Rushmer, R., & Davies, H. T. O. (2004). Unlearning in health care. Quality & Safety in Health Care, 13(suppl 2), ii10–ii15.
7. Hoff, T. (2011). Deskilling and adaptation among primary care physicians using two work innovations. Health Care Management Review, 36(4), 338–348.
8. Ong, W. K., & Chan, C. S. (2025). Maverick++: Collaboration-free unlearning for medical privacy preservation in healthcare federated systems. IEEE Access, 13, 165441–165455. https://doi.org/10.1109/ACCESS.2025.3611992
9. Acosta, J. N., Falcone, G. J., Rajpurkar, P., & Topol, E. J. (2022, September). Multimodal biomedical AI. Nature Medicine, 28(9), 1773–1784.
10. Huang, S.-C., Pareek, A., Seyyedi, S., Banerjee, I., & Lungren, M. (2020). Fusion of medical imaging and electronic health records using deep learning: A systematic review and implementation guidelines. NPJ Digital Medicine, 3, 12.

11. Sakib, S. K., & Xie, M. (2024, November). Machine unlearning in digital healthcare: Addressing technical and ethical challenges. In Proceedings of the AAAI Symposium Series (Vol. 4, No. 1, pp. 319–322).
12. Koch, K., & Soll, M. (2023). No matter how you slice it: Machine unlearning with sisa comes at the expense of minority classes. In 2023 IEEE Conference on Secure and Trustworthy Machine Learning (SaTML) (pp. 622–637). IEEE.
13. Paranjape, K., Schinkel, M., Panday, R. N., Car, J., & Nanayakkara, P. (2019). Introducing artificial intelligence training in medical education. JMIR Medical Education, 5(2), e16048.
14. Doshi-Velez, F., & Kim, B. (2017). Toward a rigorous science of interpretable machine learning. arXiv Preprint arXiv:1702.08608.
15. Sculley, D., Holt, G., Golovin, D., Davydov, E., Phillips, T., Ebner, D., Chaudhary, V., Young, M., Crespo, J.-F., & Dennison, D. (2015). Hidden technical debt in machine learning systems. Advances in Neural Information Processing Systems, 28.
16. Deng, Z., Luo, L., & Chen, H. (2024). Enable the right to be forgotten with federated client unlearning in medical imaging. arXiv preprint arXiv:2407.02356.
17. Nasirigerdeh, R., Razmi, N., Schnabel, J. A., Rueckert, D., & Kaissis, G. (2024). Machine unlearning for medical imaging. arXiv preprint arXiv:2407.07539.
18. Ge, L. (2024). Erasing memories: Implementing client unlearning in medical image analysis. In International Conference on Image Processing and Artificial Intelligence (ICIPAl 2024) (Vol. 13213, pp. 955–960). SPIE.
19. Zhou, J., Li, T., Fong, S. J., Dey, N., & Crespo, R. G. (2023). Exploring chatGPT'S potential for consultation, recommendations and report diagnosis: Gastric cancer and gastroscopy reports' case. IJIMAI, 8(2), 7–13.
20. Patel, S., Gayakvad, B., Solanki, R., Patel, R., & Khunt, D. (2023). Toward the digitization of healthcare record management. Human–Machine Interface: Making Healthcare Digital, 411–447.
21. Chen, P.-T., Lin, C.-L., & Wu, W.-N. (2020). Big data management in healthcare: Adoption challenges and implications. International Journal of Information Management, 53, 102078.
22. Hafner, J. H. (2016, January). Does incomplete unlearning impact medical errors? In 2016 49th Hawaii International Conference on System Sciences (HICSS) (pp. 4324–4333). IEEE.
23. Lindstrom, C. (2024). Federated unlearning in financial applications. https://doi.org/10.20944/preprints202409.1816.v2
24. Brodzinski, C. E. (2024). Survey of security and data attacks on machine unlearning in financial and e-commerce. arXiv preprint arXiv:2410.00055.
25. Qi, C. (2024). Graph unlearning: Mechanism and future direction for machine unlearning with complex relationships. https://doi.org/10.20944/preprints202409.1733.v1
26. Milner, L. (2024). Threat models to machine unlearning. https://doi.org/10.20944/preprints202409.2068.v1
27. Zhang, D., Pan, S., Hoang, T., Xing, Z., Staples, M., Xu, X., . . . & Zhu, L. (2024). To be forgotten or to be fair: Unveiling fairness implications of machine unlearning methods. AI and Ethics, 4(1), 83–93.
28. Shaik, T., Tao, X., Xie, H., Li, L., Zhu, X., & Li, Q. (2024). Exploring the landscape of machine unlearning: A comprehensive survey and taxonomy. IEEE Transactions on Neural Networks and Learning Systems, 36(7), 11676–11696. https://doi.org/10.1109/TNNLS.2024.3486109
29. Lin, H. C., & Yang, S. H. (2023, July). Using shadow models to protect private data on machine unlearning. In 2023 International Conference on Consumer Electronics-Taiwan (ICCE-Taiwan) (pp. 687–688). IEEE.

30. Tang, L., & Joshi, J. (2024, October). Toward privacy-preserving and secure machine unlearning: Taxonomy, challenges and research directions. In 2024 IEEE 6th International Conference on Trust, Privacy and Security in Intelligent Systems, and Applications (TPS-ISA) (pp. 280–291). IEEE.
31. Li, N., Zhou, C., Gao, Y., Chen, H., Zhang, Z., Kuang, B., & Fu, A. (2025). Machine unlearning: Taxonomy, metrics, applications, challenges, and prospects. IEEE Transactions on Neural Networks and Learning Systems, 36(8), 13709–13729. https://doi.org/10.1109/TNNLS.2025.3530988
32. Dige, O., Singh, D., Yau, T. F., Zhang, Q., Bolandraftar, B., Zhu, X., & Khattak, F. K. (2024). Mitigating social biases in language models through unlearning. arXiv preprint arXiv:2406.13551.
33. Lu, H., Isonuma, M., Mori, J., & Sakata, I. (2024). Toward transfer unlearning: Empirical evidence of cross-domain bias mitigation. arXiv preprint arXiv:2407.16951.

6 Data Privacy Ethical Implications

6.1 RIGHT TO BE FORGOTTEN

Artificial intelligence (AI) has developed rapidly over the past three decades, changing the nature of work of all industries and daily living [1]. Another key factor that has contributed to this boom is machine learning, especially a potent subfield known as deep learning [2]. In deep learning, massive data volumes are fed into specific algorithms that consist of several layers of neural networks. These networks are trained to recognize patterns within the information and are then capable of applying those patterns to both classify information (such as recognizing a face or sorting emails) and produce novel information (such as creating an image or writing a sentence) [2].

The digital environment today is overwhelmed by personal information/data/content (our photos and messages, medical, financial records, etc.). This enormous availability of data is enabled by significant advancements in data storage and transmission technology, which can enable systems to collect, store, and manipulate personal information at an enormous scale [3]. Present-day AI tools are effective demonstrations of deep learning in action: facial recognition systems; image-generating models, such as DALL-E and Midjourney; large language models, such as GPT-4, Bard, and ChatGPT; or even deepfakes, which can be highly persuasive fakes of real people [4]. Each of them is based on deep learning models that are trained to learn to perceive patterns in the input data. These models use weights and biases as parameters that determine the learning process. During training, these parameters are manipulated with the use of large datasets, which allows the model to yield the correct prediction or produce believable outputs. Models are often large but typically have fewer parameters than the overall size of the data on which they are trained; thus, they act as compact statistical examples of that data instead of as models that store it [5].

6.1.1 Reasons Behind the Increase in the Right to Be Forgotten

With increasing global internet penetration and the increased use of sophisticated AI and machine learning products, vast quantities of personal information are being gathered and processed [6]: information that we seek on the internet, purchases, our location, or even the shapes of our faces can tell us a lot about our identity, our likes, and how we socialize with people (Figure 6.1). Owing to this, personal information has become very valuable not only to businesses but also to politics [7].

In some cases, however, an individual may desire to fully erase a chunk of his or her data—which is something that at one time was appropriate to share but no longer

DOI: 10.1201/9781003771470-6

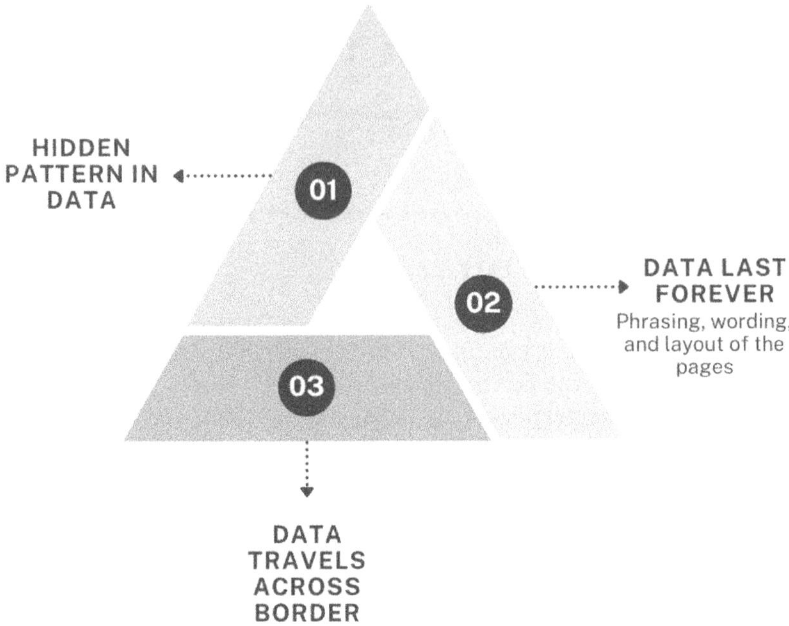

FIGURE 6.1 Reasons behind the increase in RTBF.

seems to fit: that is easier said than done. AI has been incorporated into nearly all industries, including healthcare, banking, and even social media. These systems are learned using past data and rely on them to operate effectively. AI works most effectively with as much data as possible; therefore, even data that were previously viewed as unimportant are stored, repurposed, and analyzed once again [8]. This complicates the process of permanently removing that information in all systems. Such modifications to data storage and utilization have a dire impact on the notion of the so-called right to be forgotten (RTBF), the idea that individuals are entitled to the right to delete their personal data once they no longer desire that they should be present. However, implementing such an idea is becoming increasingly difficult for several reasons:

1. **Data last forever:** It is now extremely inexpensive and easy to store data. Consequently, businesses and organizations are inclined to retain all that they gather, in many cases, indefinitely. This implies that despite their desire to remove your information, it may still be stored in a backup, database, or cloud server [9].
2. **Hidden patterns in data:** Modern AI systems are remarkably skilled at assembling small, seemingly insignificant, pieces of data about a person, such as what that person does online or what he or she buys, and deduce far more intimate details about that person. This complicates the process of understanding what information exactly should be removed, as even minor details can be disclosing sensitive information.

3. **Data travel across borders:** The internet is indifferent to national borders. A person's information might be saved on the servers in a foreign nation where other privacy laws exist. This is because even if, according to local laws, that person's data is supposed to be deleted, it may still be held or used somewhere outside of the jurisdiction of those laws.

It is not difficult to delete personal information off a server, but it is far more challenging to do the same off AI systems. The reason is that AI models are trained on previous data, including personal data, and they are known to recall what they have learned.

In the past, it was easy to delete personal data. However, in the context of AI and machine learning, the process has become complex. These models are constructed in an unpredictable manner. An AI model is modified once it has been trained on the use of data. Therefore, the following question is posed: whether the AI model should also be altered if personal data are deleted, since the model is influenced by that data. Moreover, with this enhancement, AI systems can merge various groups of data and even make assumptions regarding confidential information that has not been provided directly [10]. The fact that data are usually stored in numerous locations around the globe with various laws worsens the issue. Technologies such as blockchain make this even more challenging, as their records are intended to be unchangeable. Large corporations such as Google and Facebook gather and retain tremendous amounts of personal information. This gives them much control over the online life of people, which may become a source of privacy issues. Thus, complete erasure of the digital traces of a person is becoming almost impossible. AI systems may retain long-term information, and in such a manner, people are unable to regulate how they are perceived online. Accordingly, now, there is a powerful necessity to reconsider the meaning of the right to be forgotten in the modern world.

6.1.2 Issues of LLMs Related to Personal Data

Large language models (LLMs) are constructed on the basis of deep neural networks with billions of parameters. These models are trained using large amounts of data, and most of this information is gathered using publicly available internet resources [11, 12]. The model learns values during training, which are referred to as weights and biases. Such values assist the system in identifying patterns among the data and subsequently apply the patterns to categorize information or create a new text.

These models have a large number of parameters; however, the size of the data utilized to train these models tends to be less than the size of the data itself. A set of parameters represents and memorizes each word or token of the training data. Moreover, every parameter can contribute to the memory of a number of various tokens. In this manner, parameters behave in a similar fashion as neurons in the human brain do. For example, when it is necessary to forget a sentence, for example, in EMILDAI [13], which is the best program for studying data protection and privacy, only a handful of the 1.7 trillion parameters of the model may be deleted. Nonetheless, one of the significant issues is that the parameters that can be associated with that sentence are not known. It is yet not clear with any degree of certainty what parameters hold what precise pieces of information. At this point, it is not possible to trace in detail or reverse the process by which a model recalls something.

Attempts have been made to achieve the goal of machine unlearning [14], where particular data can be removed without resetting up the complete model. However, as the original information is frequently very deeply embedded into the model and reused during training, wiping it out is virtually impossible. With LLMs and generative AI, the output is produced on the basis of statistical patterns as well as relationships in the previous data that have been learned. Assuming that such personal information appeared in the training data before a deletion request, the model may still be able to make guesses, reconstruct, or guess such information when requested [15]. In contrast to other previous models such as ELMo and BERT, more recent LLMs have been created to be more user interactive with their prompts. This transformation implies that the users are currently anticipated to learn how the models operate to receive the right responses. More advanced models, such as InstructGPT and ChatGPT, have been trained with human feedback to become more competent at following human instructions [16]. During this process, a manual evaluation of responses was conducted and used to train a reward system and direct the model via a process known as reinforcement learning from human feedback. Consequently, the models have been designed such that they react better to the instructions given by the users.

Despite the common perception of LLMs as spectacular and even disruptive technologies, they are confronted with significant issues with respect to data management. Hallucination and memorization of training data are two reasons of concern.

1. **Training data memorization:** LLMs occasionally memorize personal information in their training sets. This information might be seen in their answers even in cases when no particular details are requested. These actions have been continuously witnessed in practice. Although companies are striving to take personal data out of training datasets, they can still exist and be trained in by the model [17].
2. **Hallucination:** Hallucination refers to inaccurate or fabricated information that is produced by LLMs. This may have occurred when necessary wrong information was not included in the initial training information. Stated differently, an LLM can give incorrect citations or make false conclusions, which are based on the idea of generative search even when presented with the right context. Even though guardrails and high-tech prompt methods are embraced to minimize such errors, hallucination is still a persistent issue.
3. **User chat history:** Chatbots are typically operated via LLMs, which are implemented as a chat interface, and the dialog is conducted via a sequence of messages instead of a few, one-off queries. Consequently, users tend to exchange more personal context when doing this. User consent is mandatory before such chat histories are gathered and used in other applications, such as training AI models [18]. Users should also be given a chance to revoke this permission anytime, and their data should then be deleted if they do not want it to be used to develop the models any more.

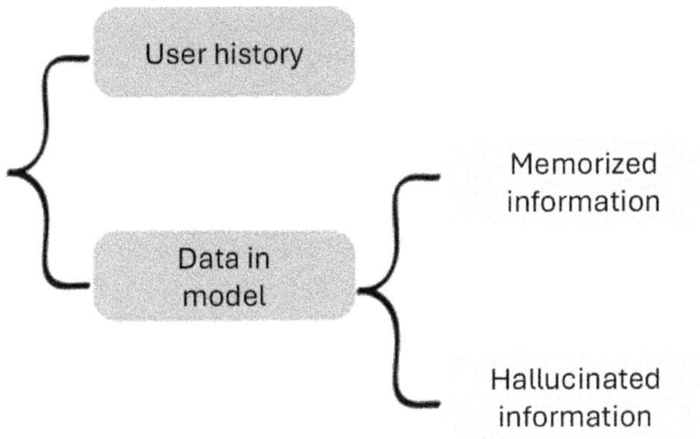

FIGURE 6.2 Situations where the rights of the data subject are applicable.

4. **In model data:** Sometimes, personal data can also be present in the model itself since they were trained on datasets that contained personal data. This hidden information can be accessed by prompts. Nevertheless, generated responses can contain both memorized personal information and distorted, hallucinated information (see Figure 6.2). Under data protection laws, such as the General Data Protection Regulation (GDPR), a person may seek access to this information, make corrections, or request that it be erased [19]. However, unfortunately, it is a significant challenge to fulfill such requests by LLMs.

Search engines have frequently been compared to LLMs. The RTBF was originally introduced in a legal case that involved search engines, whereas the magnitude of the current AI-driven systems would greatly complicate implementation. For example, GPT-4 has approximately 1.8 trillion parameters and was trained on a petabyte dataset. The model continuously reuses this enormous amount of data to identify a pattern and make a prediction; it is almost impossible to entirely eliminate the data related to a particular individual [20]. Furthermore, the products created with the help of personal data can be extensively copied and redistributed in an unmonitored and uncontrollable manner, which complicates the process of RTBF implementation. Although one might have been able to have his or her data removed from the training data, it would probably be impossible to find and delete all the outputs that had already been created and disseminated using the said data.

6.1.3 The Origin and Development of the Right to Be Forgotten

As Web 2.0 has grown, with an emphasis on social interaction, there has been a change in the societal perception of remembering and forgetting [21]. Memory has become the rule, and forgetting has become the exception. This advancement has been further accelerated by the introduction of Web 3.0, where applications and platforms have been created to gather, structure, and analyze extensive data to tailor user experiences [22]. This has led to the increased collection and distribution of personal data and the devaluation of the importance of forgetting. This trend has been enhanced by the application of machine learning. Owing to its ability to handle large volumes of data, ML has enabled the construction of profiles detailing an individual person on the basis of all their actions on the internet. The next generations of the internet, including Web 4.0, which is concerned with deeper human–machine interactions, and Web 5.0 and 6.0, which are set to imply even more intelligent and autonomous systems, are coming very soon [23]. These trends indicate that there will be increased personal data that are analyzed and integrated into digital systems.

To counteract this, the law has come in to safeguard the privacy of the individual. The concept of individuals possessing the right to their personal data was legitimized by laws such as the European Union's GDPR [24]. Article 17 of the GDPR provides individuals with the right to demand that their personal information be erased and that organizations (data controllers) comply, provided that one meets some conditions. Although this RTBF has been the key point of the GDPR mission, the total removal of the shared information on the internet is a significant challenge in practice.

A significant increase in data erasure requests has been observed since the inception of the GDPR to large platforms such as search engines and social media platforms [25]. Although GDPR was intended to be considered international in order to regulate international data transfer, the different interpretations of the regulations in different countries and the development of data-hosting zones that are not subject to EU jurisdiction have complicated its enforcement. Nevertheless, the establishment of the RTFB was a significant change in the way the law considers privacy and personal control in the digital era.

The right offered by article 17 is typically referred to as the RTBF. Such rights have been regarded as basic human rights in most legal systems. Although controversy remains as to whether it should be promoted to the status of a fundamental right in and of itself, RTBF has come to be regarded as a significant component of data protection legislation because of the values it promotes, including those of privacy, personal control, and reputation. The privacy of personal information has been regarded in Europe and most other parts of the world as one of the fundamental human rights. This right is also directly associated with the wider notion of privacy, which is ensured in the Charter of Fundamental Rights of the European Union. The rights of privacy comprise a range of guarantees, which include the right to bodily integrity, confidentiality in communication, home protection, and privilege to personal information. Although data protection and privacy rights differ in their application and justification, one can identify the connection between the RTBF and privacy rights, particularly under the conditions when the data that are to be erased are related to the personal life of a person and the demand to erase the data satisfies the legal definition of interference into his or her privacy [26]. By doing so, the RTBF acts as a protection of human rights in several ways. Although its legalization was regarded as a significant move toward granting people the power to manage their personal data, the method of implementing and enforcing the law in practice has been challenging and complicated.

6.2 TOWARD A MULTIFACETED STRATEGY

To ensure that the RTBF is more sustainable and effective in the future, a middle ground should be established. This would entail some parts collaborating with each other:

1. Amendments to the laws and international agreements must be proposed such that the removal of cross-border data is treated more comprehensively and the existing gaps in the laws can be eliminated.
2. Privacy should be considered by the use of new technologies such as machine unlearning, secure multiparty computation, and temporary (ephemeral) encryption to alter the way data are stored, manipulated, and erased.
3. The implementation of policies and systems of governance must be executed in a collaborative approach with governments, tech firms, and civil society such that the rules can be revised on a regular basis during constant deliberations.
4. Ethical checks and monitoring should be included to ensure that individual privacy rights are protected while still allowing certain information to be kept for the public good—such as for history, journalism, or education.

By combining these efforts, the next version of the RTBF can be built in a way that is practical, fair, and forward looking.

6.3 RECOMMENDATIONS TO MAINTAIN DATA PRIVACY

1. **Establish an international data privacy consortium:** There is a possibility to establish an international data privacy consortium on the basis of the existing efforts of organizations such as the Organisation for Economic Co-operation and Development, Asia-Pacific Economic Cooperation, and the Council of Europe. With the help of such a consortium, the global standards of the RTBF might be established, cross-border disputes might be solved, and the consistency of practices in their enforcement might be achieved.
2. **Mandate machine unlearning protocols:** Machine unlearning protocols should be mandatory for developers of AI. These standards would enable certain data components to be deleted from models without affecting the system ethically. To make this possible, it would be necessary to make new investments in research and increase the collaboration between industries.
3. **Enhance funding for data protection authorities:** More funding should be provided to data protection authorities so that they are better equipped to perform technical reviews, impose penalties where necessary, and work more effectively with international counterparts.
4. **Develop tiered data categories:** A tiered classification system for data could be introduced, where different types of data—such as personal, sensitive, or historical data—are treated with different levels of care. This would assist in ensuring that the deletion of data is performed in a careful manner and depending on its nature and usage.

5. **Promote corporate transparency and accountability:** Companies can be encouraged or mandated to be more transparent and accountable by conducting privacy impact assessments, publishing data usage maps, and disclosing how effectively they are meeting privacy regulations.
6. **Educate and empower individuals:** People can be educated and empowered by means of digital literacy programs that make people aware of their rights in data and the potential risks of sharing data, as well as how to make successful requests to have their data deleted.

REFERENCES

1. Russell, S., & Norvig, P. (2020). *Artificial Intelligence: A Modern Approach* (4th ed.). Pearson.
2. Goodfellow, I., Bengio, Y., & Courville, A. (2016). *Deep Learning.* MIT Press.
3. Oussous, A., Benjelloun, F. Z., Ait Lahcen, A., & Belfkih, S. (2018). Big data technologies: A survey. *Journal of King Saud University-Computer and Information Sciences*, 30(4), 431–448.
4. OpenAI. (2023). *GPT-4 Technical Report.* https://openai.com/research/gpt-4
5. Carlini, N., Tramer, F., Wallace, E., Jagielski, M., Herbert-Voss, A., Lee, K., . . . & Song, D. (2021). Extracting training data from large language models. In *USENIX Security Symposium.*
6. Floridi, L., & Taddeo, M. (2016). What is data ethics? *Philosophical Transactions of the Royal Society A*, 374(2083), 20160360.
7. Zuboff, S. (2019). *The Age of Surveillance Capitalism.* PublicAffairs.
8. Rocher, L., Hendrickx, J. M., & de Montjoye, Y. A. (2019). Estimating the success of reidentifications in incomplete datasets using generative models. *Nature Communications*, 10(1), 1–9.
9. Mayer-Schönberger, V. (2011). *Delete: The Virtue of Forgetting in the Digital Age.* Princeton University Press.
10. Carlini, N., Tramer, F., Wallace, E., Jagielski, M., Herbert-Voss, A., Lee, K., . . . & Song, D. (2021). Extracting training data from large language models. In *USENIX Security Symposium.*
11. Bommasani, R., Hudson, D. A., Adeli, E., et al. (2021). On the opportunities and risks of foundation models. arXiv preprint arXiv:2108.07258.
12. Khosravy, M., Gupta, N., Dey, N., & Witkowski, O. (2025, February). Are LLMs ready to shoulder biomedical trust? In *International Conference on Innovations in Biotechnology and Health Sciences* (pp. 125–142). Singapore: Springer Nature Singapore.
13. https://emildai.eu/eternal-sunshine-of-the-mechanical-mind-machine-learning-vs-the-right-to-be-forgotten/
14. Gupta, S., Naskar, A., Misra, B., S, H. K., Chakraborty, S., & Kulkarni, A. S. (2025). Integrating k-Means++ with ARCANE: A scalable framework for exact cluster unlearning. In *Proceedings of the Seventh International Conference on Research in Computational Intelligence and Communication Networks (ICRCICN 2025)* (pp. 418–423). IEEE.
15. Bourtoule, L., Chandrasekaran, V., Choquette-Choo, C. A., et al. (2021). Machine unlearning. In *IEEE Symposium on Security and Privacy* (pp. 141–159).
16. Hou, J., Li, T., Fong, S. J., Dey, N., & Crespo, R. G. (2023). Exploring chatGPT'S potential for consultation, recommendations and report diagnosis: Gastric cancer and gastroscopy reports' case. IJIMAI, 8(2), 7–13.

17. Carlini, N., Liu, C., Erlingsson, Ú., Kos, J., & Song, D. (2019). The secret sharer: Measuring unintended neural network memorization & extracting secrets. In *USENIX Security Symposium* (pp. 267–284).
18. Veale, M., & Borgesius, F. Z. (2021). Demystifying the draft EU artificial intelligence act. *Computer Law Review International*, 22(4), 97–112.
19. Wachter, S., Mittelstadt, B., & Floridi, L. (2017). Why a right to explanation of automated decision-making does not exist in the general data protection regulation. *International Data Privacy Law*, 7(2), 76–99.
20. Kroll, J. A., Huey, J., Barocas, S., Felten, E. W., Reidenberg, J. R., Robinson, D. G., & Yu, H. (2017). Accountable algorithms. *University of Pennsylvania Law Review*, 165(3), 633–705.
21. Mayer-Schönberger, V. (2009). *Delete: The Virtue of Forgetting in the Digital Age.* Princeton University Press.
22. Spiekermann, S. (2015). *Ethical IT Innovation: A Value-Based System Design Approach.* Taylor & Francis.
23. Aghila, G., & Rajalakshmi, S. (2020). Evolution of web technologies: Web 1.0 to Web 6.0. *International Journal of Computer Science and Mobile Applications*, 8(2), 1–7.
24. European Parliament and Council. (2016). *Regulation (EU) 2016/679 (General Data Protection Regulation).* Official Journal of the European Union.
25. Rosen, J. (2012). The right to be forgotten. *Stanford Law Review Online*, 64, 88–92.
26. Toth, A. (2021). The right to be forgotten: Data protection and beyond. *Computer Law & Security Review*, 41, 105536.

7 Challenges in Applying RTBF to AI Systems

7.1 CHALLENGES IN APPLYING RTBF

In the digital age, gigatons of information are created and processed by machine learning algorithms on a second-by-second basis to make correct and timely decisions. However, situations always exist in which a user may want to remove a piece of information that is no longer necessary or applicable as it used to be. Even though it is relatively easy to delete such data off of the backend servers, it is significantly more complicated to erase all the data completely out of artificial intelligence systems because such models of the system, by definition, are prone to retaining information once it has been integrated into the training. This continuity provokes serious issues of privacy and security, especially in a world where individual information is shared through online platforms all the time. In addition to these issues, users normally desire temporally relevant recommendations, as opposed to past and irrelevant information.

In its General Data Protection Regulation (GDPR), the European Union has resolved these problems with a concept known as the right to be forgotten (RTBF). Nevertheless, in reality, it is difficult to retract the information distributed on various online platforms. When applied to AI, deleting data that was used to train the model may frequently require retraining this model, which is both computationally intensive and resource intensive. This leads to one serious question: which methods can organizations implement to successfully eliminate user information in AI systems when they revoke their consent but which at the same time prevents the need to resolve the prohibitive costs of retraining the entire model?

7.2 TECHNICAL CHALLENGES

Data replication is among the most significant technical issues in the implementation of the RTBF for AI systems. In practice, data are often copied and kept in various infrastructures, such as backup servers and cloud servers, making it difficult to ensure that they are completely erased. The decentralized design of current AI systems, especially those that use blockchain or distributed computing, further complicates the deletion process, which can be spread over all global networks of nodes, making it almost impossible to completely eliminate [1]. The use of anonymization, which is used as a means of protecting personal information, creates more complexity. Although the RTBF does not apply to anonymized data under the GDPR, the anonymization methods are not entirely reliable. The development of machine learning has made it possible to reidentify individuals in anonymized data by cross-linking them with other related data, which invalidates anonymization as a strong privacy protection tool [2].

 DOI: 10.1201/9781003771470-7

Even where organizations are willing to abide by deletion requests, there are usually technical challenges that make it difficult to do so completely:

1. **Data redundancy:** Data redundancy is ensured when more than one copy of data is saved to facilitate reliability and reduce latency [3].
2. **Server-side caching:** The information on a cache on web applications is kept to maximize performance; therefore, it is not possible to erase it instantly [4].
3. **Blockchain immutability:** The immutability principle of decentralized systems is used to ensure that there is no chance of removing it without forking the blockchain [5].

In addition, machine learning pipelines are usually characterized by a sequence of processing, transformation, and aggregation stages. A single bit of personal information can be irreversibly perplexed into derived datasets or model parameters; thus, it is more difficult to remove.

7.3 CONCEPTUAL CHALLENGES

In addition to technical barriers, AI systems face conceptual barriers in their definition of personal data. The definition of personal data in the GDPR is extremely broad, as it refers to any information concerning an identified or identifiable natural person. However, within the framework of AI, the line between personal and nonpersonal data shifts rather often. Although the models are not directly associated with identifiable persons, the insights or predictions made through them may also have privacy concerns, which are also addressed in the RTBF [6].

This is complex because AI models are dynamic. Models are continuously evolving and growing over time with new data; therefore, the effects and influences of the information of a singular person are incorporated into the parameters of the models and, therefore, are not very easy to eliminate. Important questions are raised regarding whether the RTBF can be extended to the outputs of AI systems, where predictions or decisions are made on the basis of personal data. In this context, the feasibility of implementing such requirements also needs to be kept in mind [7].

7.4 ETHICAL CONCERNS RELATED TO AI INFERENCES

Artificial intelligence systems have an incredible ability to predict sensitive attributes on the basis of little data, an aspect that imposes some deep ethical concerns. Take the situation whereby a person asks for the deletion of data concerning political affiliations or health status. Although such data are eliminated, the model still might have latent patterns, which can be used in the future to infer such attributes.

- **Inference of sensitive attributes:** Since algorithms are trained on large-scale datasets, they can identify correlations between a racial or sexual orientation or a religious belief when these attributes are not introduced [8].

- **Stigmatization and discrimination:** Once identified, these qualities can be used to perform selective advertising or discrimination, thus defeating the intent of erasure itself [9].

7.5 JURISDICTIONAL AND CROSS-BORDER DATA FLOWS

The data flows are not limited by national borders, which makes it difficult to implement privacy rights. The extraterritoriality of laws such as the GDPR is an effort to address this transnational situation, but there are still contradictions between laws. Some jurisdictions have adopted a more lenient stance on freedom of expression and thus restrict takedown demands, whereas others have lower data protection values, which is effectively a safe haven where companies can be spared the task of trying to meet the stringent requirements of full erasure [10]. In a globally networked world, those seeking erasure must frequently negotiate complex, multijurisdictional legal procedures [11]. The RTBF is still virtually unattainable to many, especially those who are not endowed with the wherewithal to fight cross-border issues.

7.6 COMMERCIAL INTERESTS AND DATA MONETIZATION

In many technology corporations, consumer information is the basis of their revenue models, which is used to drive advertising and predictive analytics [12]. This places a burden on personal choice with respect to personal data erasure and corporate motivation to keep it. The erase requests are expensive and have complicated technicalities, thus leading to poor or sluggish compliance. These economic deterrents demolish the timeliness to overwrite significant data.

7.7 SOCIETAL AND CULTURAL IMPLICATIONS

The cross-border implementation of the RTBF is faced with two broader interests in society at large to protect historical records, cultural heritage, and freedom of information [13]. Types of journalism, scholarly research, and archives are founded on the principle that the information must be accessible to the populace to create knowledge [14]. Freedom to erase may deteriorate such common interests, leading to discussions about whether some types of information (historical events, data about famous personalities, etc.) should ever be lost at all.

7.8 STOCHASTICITY OF TRAINING

Unlearning becomes even more complex because of the stochastic nature of machine learning training. Neural network training is usually performed on random mini-batches of videos of fixed size, and the sequence of batches is randomized [15]. This randomness blocks the exact effect of individual data points on the model, making it difficult to selectively wipe the sample across every training run.

7.9 INCREMENTALITY OF TRAINING

Model training is a naturally incremental process, implying that the modification produced by one data sample affects the performance of a model [15]. Similarly, previous training data determine the performance on a particular sample. Eliminating the downstream implications of a given training sample therefore poses a daunting problem for machine unlearning because its impact spreads throughout the learning process of the model.

7.10 CATASTROPHIC UNLEARNING

In practice, unlearned models usually perform worse than models retrained on leftover data do [16, 17]. This degradation may increase exponentially as more and more of the data are erased, a phenomenon also commonly known as catastrophic unlearning [16]. Although some studies [18] have provided mitigation measures, including the design of specialized loss functions, natural and robust mechanisms that prevent catastrophic unlearning have yet to be identified.

7.11 CHALLENGES OF APPLYING RTBF TO LLMS

With regard to the format of the data, the RTBF can be applied to two types of data: the user chat history and the in-model data, which can be further categorized into memorized data and hallucinated information.

7.11.1 User Chat History

As mentioned previously, these LLMs are built into chatbots that interact with users in an anthropomorphic and conversational manner, which can retrieve more personal information from users.

7.11.2 In-Model Data

This type of data includes memorized and hallucinated data. The theoretically removable data, which are based on training corpora, can be memorized. Information that has been hallucinated is more challenging to erase but can be erased or corrected by law as part of the rights to erasure and rectification. The fact that the mechanisms of LLM are opaque also complicates access to the memorized and hallucinated data, and the practical implementation of RTBF becomes especially complicated.

7.12 COMPUTATIONAL EXPENSE

Unlearning is often linked to high computational costs, particularly in cases when the original training data are large. Moreover, the process has the effect of overfitting; that is, the model is too specialized for the remaining training data and renders it ineffective at extrapolating to new, unseen inputs.

7.13 LOSS OF IMPORTANT INFORMATION

The deletion of information may accidentally result in the disappearance of useful information. For example, to remove bias related to a given demographic group, it might be necessary to remove all examples, including those related to that demographic group, thereby also removing important information used in prediction models. Close consideration of the effect of unlearning on the performance of the models is thus necessary. To achieve fairness and accuracy without reducing predictive utility, complementary plans, including the diversity of training data, might be necessary.

7.14 LACK INTERPRETABILITY

The nature of contemporary machine learning models, which involve high complexity and a considerable number of interdependent parameters, features, and so forth, complicates unlearning outcome prediction. A change or the removal of one parameter may have unwanted ripple effects on a model. In particular, deep learning models have low interpretability, making it difficult to determine which elements should be unlearned and their impact on overall performance.

7.15 ENHANCING THE PUBLIC UNDERSTANDING OF RTBF AND AI

Another significant issue with regard to the successful implementation of RTBF in AI systems is the creation of public awareness. Some individuals do not even realize the extent to which their data are utilized or their rights per frameworks such as the GDPR or the Central Consumer Protection Authority (CCPA). This gap can be bridged by carrying out educational campaigns that will inform the population about AI activities, the importance of RTBF, and how to assert their rights [19]. Ethical advice is also required to avoid the application of RTBF in a way that will hamper innovation through privacy. To develop ethical implications of RTBF in AI, it is possible to conduct public consultations and ethical reviews of technologists, ethicists, policymakers, and citizens to gain a thorough understanding of the problem.

7.16 BALANCING PRIVACY RIGHTS WITH THE BENEFITS OF AI

Although RTBF is a rather important privacy protection method, the adoption of practice should be balanced with the benefits of AI to society. Mechanisms of AI are very advantageous to the health, security, and efficiency sectors. Such improvements may not be possible because the implementation of RTBF may be too stringent. Regulators and policymakers should consider the creation of legal frameworks in which privacy is ensured but does not prevent responsible AI use. This may incorporate safe harbors and exemptions to some forms of AI processing, which may be carried out in the common good interest, provided that appropriate protection is taken [20].

7.17 HYPERPARAMETER SEARCH

Unlearning methods may include sharding and slicing, and as such, their applicability may frequently necessitate a reevaluation of the hyperparameter choices made on the entire dataset. As an example, the number of training epochs or batches can be varied. Each of the constituent models may need a varied set of hyperparameters to yield the best results when multiple slices are employed. As the number of models increases, hyperparameter tuning becomes an extremely challenging task and presents serious computational challenges.

7.18 UNCERTAINTY

Deliberate deletion of knowledge within neural networks leads to various forms of ambiguity, which can compromise the stability, generalizability, and reliability of the models.

- **Epistemic uncertainty:** This refers to the partial information on the underlying data distribution underlying the model. Wipeout of some training points may add uncertainty and disturb predictions [21, 22]. Methods have been proposed to measure the differences in model parameters between unlearning and a retrained model.
- **Aleatoric uncertainty:** This is caused by the randomness of the data. Unlearning has the ability to modify the variance of parameters, which influences predictive consistency. Research has shown that unlearning processes that use gradient ascent can actually increase aleatoric uncertainty unless suitable regularization tools are used.

REFERENCES

1. Veale, M., Binns, R., & Ausloos, J. (2018). When data protection by design and data subject rights clash. International Data Privacy Law, 8(2), 105–123.
2. Narayanan, A., & Shmatikov, V. (2010). Myths and fallacies of "personally identifiable information". Communications of the ACM, 53(6), 24–26.
3. Pearson, S., & Benameur, A. (2010, November). Privacy, security and trust issues arising from cloud computing. In 2010 IEEE Second International Conference on Cloud Computing Technology and Science (pp. 693–702). IEEE.
4. Halder, D., & Jaishankar, K. (2016). Celebrities and cyber crimes: An analysis of the victimization of female film stars on the internet. Temida, 19(3–4), 355–372.
5. Finck, M. (2018). Blockchains: Regulating the unknown. German Law Journal, 19(4), 665–692.
6. Tene, O., & Polonetsky, J. (2012). Big data for all: Privacy and user control in the age of analytics. Northwestern Journal of Technology & Intellectual Property, 11, 239.
7. Wachter, S., Mittelstadt, B., & Floridi, L. (2017). Why a right to explanation of automated decision-making does not exist in the general data protection regulation. International Data Privacy Law, 7(2), 76–99.
8. Kosinski, M., Stillwell, D., & Graepel, T. (2013). Private traits and attributes are predictable from digital records of human behavior. Proceedings of the National Academy of Sciences, 110(15), 5802–5805.

9. Barocas, S., & Selbst, A. D. (2016). Big data's disparate impact. California Law Review, 104, 671.
10. Schwartz, P. M., & Solove, D. J. (2014). Reconciling personal information in the United States and European Union. California Law Review, 102, 877.
11. Svantesson, D. J. B. (2013). A "layered approach" to the extraterritoriality of data privacy laws. International Data Privacy Law, 3(4), 278–286.
12. Zuboff, S. (2019, January). Surveillance capitalism and the challenge of collective action. In New labor forum (Vol. 28, No. 1, pp. 10–29). Sage, CA and Los Angeles, CA: Sage Publications.
13. Richards, N., & Hartzog, W. (2015). Taking trust seriously in privacy law. Stanford Technology Law Review, 19, 431.
14. Rosen, M. (2012). Dignity: Its history and meaning. Harvard University Press.
15. Bourtoule, L., Chandrasekaran, V., Choquette-Choo, C. A., Jia, H., Travers, A., Zhang, B., . . . & Papernot, N. (2021, May). Machine unlearning. In 2021 IEEE Symposium on Security and Privacy (SP) (pp. 141–159). IEEE.
16. Nguyen, Q. P., Low, B. K. H., & Jaillet, P. (2020). Variational Bayesian unlearning. Advances in Neural Information Processing Systems, 33, 16025–16036.
17. Nguyen, Q. P., Oikawa, R., Divakaran, D. M., Chan, M. C., & Low, B. K. H. (2022, May). Markov chain Monte Carlo-based machine unlearning: Unlearning what needs to be forgotten. In Proceedings of the 2022 ACM on Asia Conference on Computer and Communications Security (pp. 351–363).
18. Golatkar, A., Achille, A., & Soatto, S. (2020, August). Forgetting outside the box: Scrubbing deep networks of information accessible from input–output observations. In European Conference on Computer Vision (pp. 383–398). Cham: Springer International Publishing.
19. Floridi, L. (2019). Translating principles into practices of digital ethics: Five risks of being unethical. Philosophy & Technology, 32(2), 185–193.
20. Mittelstadt, B. D., Allo, P., Taddeo, M., Wachter, S., & Floridi, L. (2016). The ethics of algorithms: Mapping the debate. Big Data & Society, 3(2), 2053951716679679.
21. Becker, A., & Liebig, T. (2022). Evaluating machine unlearning via epistemic uncertainty. arXiv preprint arXiv:2208.10836.
22. Chan, M. A., Molina, M. J., & Metzler, C. A. (2024). Estimating epistemic and aleatoric uncertainty with a single model. Advances in Neural Information Processing Systems, 37, 109845–109870.

8 Conclusions and Future Research Directions

8.1 FUTURE RESEARCH TRAJECTORIES

In this chapter, current and potential developments in machine unlearning [1] are analyzed, and the findings are summarized.

8.1.1 Influence Functions Are the Dominant Methods

Understanding the impact of a given data item on a model's parameters or model performance is the key to machine unlearning. Such insights accelerate the unlearning process immensely by simply reversing the model updates associated with the target data. Although there could be some offset in doing so, promising results have shown that this offset can be bounded [2].

8.1.2 Reachability of the Model Parameters

Existing works define unlearning as obtaining a new model with an accuracy as good as if the model had been retrained without the data to be forgotten [3]. It is clear that such a parameter space assumption should be considered. As model parameters can be reachable with or without certain data, questions have been raised regarding cases where the original and unlearned models share identical parameters. Although some studies [4] use parameter distributions to address this problem, there could still be false positive cases, where some effects from the forgotten data still exist in the unlearned model.

8.1.3 Unlearning Verification (Data Auditing)

Unlearning verification (or data auditing) is the process of determining whether specific data have been eliminated from a model. To fully enable regulations over the RTBF, the unlearning effect should be independently verified. There have been only a few works on unlearning verification [5]. However, the definition of successful verification is still controversial, as different unlearning solutions use different evaluation metrics, especially when the cutoff threshold of a verification metric still depends on the application domain [6].

8.1.4 Federated Unlearning

Federated Unlearning provides a unique setting for machine unlearning research [7]. It has separate clients who participate in the federated training process. As a result,

DOI: 10.1201/9781003771470-8

removing a client from the federation could be performed precisely via historical updates. The rationale behind this is that the user data on a client mostly help to make correct predictions about that user. This locality helps to avoid a catastrophic unlearning phenomenon in a traditional machine learning setting. However, one should consider instances in federated learning where the data are non-independent and identically distributed (non-IID) or where removal requests affect a subset of the data of a client.

8.1.5 Model Repair by Unlearning

Adversarial attacks have been proven to poison machine learning models. Intuitively, if poisonous data are detected and removed and then the model is retrained, the new model should be poison free. However, retraining would be too expensive. This is indeed similar to the unlearning setting. Unlike existing defense methods, machine learning models determine and then update the inner problematic weights through influence functions. Current research on fairness and debiased learning focuses on learning a fair and unbiased feature representation [8], where machine unlearning, for example, feature unlearning [9], allows for the correct removal of biased features while maintaining model quality.

8.1.6 Proposed Changes to the GDPR and CCPA to Better Address the AI Challenge

The current legal frameworks under the GDPR and CCPA are not specifically designed with AI in mind, which creates challenges in applying RTBF to these systems. One potential adjustment to the GDPR could involve clearer guidelines on how RTBF should be applied to AI-generated data, particularly in cases where personal data have been transformed or anonymized. Additionally, the GDPR could introduce specific provisions for AI, requiring companies to develop data deletion protocols that are technically feasible and effective. With respect to the CCPA, which currently provides more limited RTBF rights than the GDPR does, a revision could involve expanding the scope of RTBF to include all forms of AI-generated data, not just those that are directly identifiable. Furthermore, both the GDPR and the CCPA could benefit from the establishment of more detailed standards for transparency and accountability in AI, ensuring that data subjects are fully informed about how their data are used in AI systems and how they can exercise their RTBF rights.

8.1.7 Unlearning for Different Data Structures

The main research work has focused on unlearning algorithms on set-structured and graph-structured training data. However, more sophisticated forms of data, such as text, speech, and multimedia, are currently being trained for models, especially in areas such as natural language processing [10] and audio/video recognition [11]. The application of unlearning methods to these various types of data is considered a key step forward, but there are major difficulties. The peculiarities of every type of data needs to be considered: timing and sequentiality in speech and language, spatial relations in images, and hierarchies in knowledge graphs. In addition, the progress of multimodal unlearning [12], which is able to work in combinations of data types, is important for facilitating real-world applications. The solution to these challenges should greatly expand the applicability of machine unlearning.

8.1.8 Unlearning for Nonconvex Models

Convolutional neural networks, recurrent neural networks, and transformers are nonconvex models that have been extensively used in various fields. However, the focus of approximate unlearning studies has been on convex models. Efficient and effective unlearning algorithms have yet to be applied to nonconvex neural networks [13]. The challenges associated with the nonconvex optimization problem include local optima and saddle points and the requirement to offer the same theoretical guarantees as those found in the convex setting. Further complications arise with the structural peculiarities of neural networks, such as activation functions and a normalization layer [14].

8.1.9 User-Specified Granularity of Unlearning

The vast majority of developed machine unlearning techniques are aimed at working at the instance level, eliminating the impact of single training cases. However, users may need finer-grained control. As an illustration, one can include a request to remove certain sensitive parts of an image and leave the rest or delete certain words in a text document that are considered unacceptable. One of the research directions is the creation of interactive and interpretable unlearning algorithms that can allow user-specified granularity. These algorithms should also be able to detect semantic components in examples and evaluate their input to model predictions. Such increased user control may greatly increase the ability of unlearning techniques to suit a wide variety of needs.

8.1.10 Privacy Assurance for Unlearning

Differential privacy has typically been used to guarantee approximate unlearning algorithms [13, 15]. Nevertheless, relative privacy budgets are frequently used in differential privacy to trade privacy and utility [16], which can be inadequate in applications that require privacy to be extremely high [17, 18]. Therefore, interest in more powerful concepts other than differential privacy has been established as a valuable line of research. Such possibilities include approaches based on information theory [19], which directly constrains the quantity of information regarding deleted data that remain in the model after unlearning. This line of work needs to overcome the challenge of extracting information from models. The use of these algorithms might be pursued to increase the interpretability and verifiability of machine learning algorithms.

8.1.11 Quantitative Evaluation Metrics

Analysis of the various unlearning approaches requires the establishment of quantifiable measures that can measure the extent of influence removal of the forgotten data and the extent of influence retention of the remaining data [20]. To construct such fine-grained metrics, a systematic analysis of the memorization processes of machine learning models on different datasets is needed [20]. There are sophisticated devices available in information theory [21] and explainability studies [22] that are believed to be useful in this endeavor. The designed metrics should help analyze machine unlearning algorithms theoretically and promote the creation and implementation of practical techniques to rely on unlearning.

8.1.12 Adversarial Machine Unlearning

Recent studies have focused more on adversarial attacks on machine learning systems as a way to improve the comprehension and security of these models [23–25]. In this situation, adversarial machine unlearning explores attacks on unlearning algorithms, and the goal is to enhance the certification of the unlearned models [26, 27]. Unlike traditional machine unlearning, which mainly assumes the ability to mitigate adversarial threats [28], adversarial machine unlearning is more demanding because it not only considers the accuracy of models but also provides privacy assurance. Notably, adversarial unlearning can function without explicit information about the learning algorithms; however, it still takes advantage of access to the unlearning process.

8.1.13 Interpretable Machine Unlearning

It is expected that the explanations given to machine unlearning will be instrumental in creating trust in human–AI relationships and allowing verification or auditing of the deleted data [29, 30]. The inverted nature of unlearning, however, is also problematic for the generalizability of available methods of explanation. The creation of methods that can explain the unlearning process, including those based on influence functions, is a research problem that has not yet been resolved [31, 32].

8.1.14 Causality in Machine Unlearning

There are occasions when large amounts of data need to be forgotten from machine learning systems despite the percentage of data that should be forgotten being relatively low. For example, millions of data items can be impacted by data pollution attacks, but a small subset can be accurately identified by human experts or advanced detection techniques [33]. When this occurs, causality analysis [34] provides an opportunity as a mechanism to automatically detect and unlearn polluted data, thus guaranteeing that the final model is free of any corrupted information.

8.1.15 Verifiable Machine Unlearning

Verifiable machine unlearning attempts to provide provisional certainties such that a model has truly forgotten certain data. Traditional methods of unlearning usually do not involve the process of users auditing or verifying that their information has been deleted. To address this drawback, Eisenhofer et al. [35] suggested a cryptographic scheme under which users can obtain evidence of appropriate data erasure. Similarly, Guo et al. [36] proposed a backdoor-assisted validation scheme, which involves the placement of invisible marks on sensitive data to enable verification without compromising model performance. With respect to verifiable machine unlearning, future studies are likely to focus more on scalability, designing machine-unlearning-resistant evaluation measures, and enhancing privacy guarantees [37, 38].

8.2 SUMMARY

Machine learning has been integrated into modern society in many ways and has been extensively applied. Today, computer systems contain so much data about individuals, and even though access to much information has facilitated great breakthroughs in artificial intelligence, especially in machine learning, it also presents a grave issue of privacy and confidence. Such information may also undermine the perception of human–AI relationships, as more people become suspicious of the way their data are collected and stored. The same concerns have led to the implementation of the concept of the RTBF, which allows users to command the removal of their personal data in machine learning models. Although it might seem that the destruction of data in backend databases is an easy task, this act on its own cannot be considered sufficient in terms of AI. Machine learning models tend to have remnants of all the previous information and remember the previous information even after it has been deleted. Recent adversarial attack examples on trained models have shown that one can determine whether particular instances or attributes are used in training, highlighting the drawbacks of traditional deletion practices.

Machine unlearning is a direct answer to this problem. Compared with traditional retraining, which is expensive and time intensive, machine unlearning provides a subtractive feature that enables models to evolve by removing unauthorized, malicious, or outdated data points without having to be retrained on the data as a whole. This would improve privacy protection in addition to improving the resistance of AI systems to adversarial exploitation.

This book presents a systematic investigation of machine unlearning methods. The overall objective is to resolve the main issues and research developments related to the conceptualization, design, and implementation of effective unlearning strategies. The book is meant to be a complete reference source to researchers and practitioners, who might require a critical introduction to machine unlearning, its theoretical concepts, design principles, removal requests, algorithms, and practical applications. In addition to summarizing the current understanding, the book draws attention to major discoveries, new trends, and emerging directions of research in areas where machine unlearning has not yet been implemented but has high potential for implementation.

REFERENCES

1. T. T. Nguyen, T. T. Huynh, Z. Ren, P. L. Nguyen, A. W. C. Liew, H. Yin, and Q. V. H. Nguyen, "A survey of machine unlearning," ACM Transactions on Intelligent Systems and Technology, vol. 16, no. 5, pp. 1–46, 2025.

2. V. S. Chundawat, A. K. Tarun, M. Mandal, and M. Kankanhalli, “Zero-shot machine unlearning,” IEEE Transactions on Information Forensics and Security, vol. 18, pp. 2345–2354, 2023.
3. A. Golatkar, A. Achille, and S. Soatto, “Eternal sunshine of the spotless net: Selective forgetting in deep networks,” in Proceedings of the IEEE/CVF conference on computer vision and pattern recognition, 2020, pp. 9304–9312.
4. C. Guo, T. Goldstein, A. Hannun, and L. Van Der Maaten, “Certified data removal from machine learning models,” *arXiv preprint arXiv:1911.03030* (2019).
5. X. Gao, X. Ma, J. Wang, Y. Sun, B. Li, S. Ji, . . . and J. Chen, “Verifi: Toward verifiable federated unlearning,” IEEE Transactions on Dependable and Secure Computing, vol. 21, no. 6, pp. 5720–5736, 2024.
6. A. Thudi, H. Jia, I. Shumailov, and N. Papernot, “On the necessity of auditable algorithmic definitions for machine unlearning,” in 31st USENIX security symposium (USENIX Security 22), 2022, pp. 4007–4022.
7. M. F. Mridha and N. Dey (Eds.), Federated Learning in Health Care Technology. Springer, 2025.
8. J. Nam, H. Cha, S. Ahn, J. Lee, and J. Shin, “Learning from failure: Debiasing classifier from biased classifier,” Advances in Neural Information Processing Systems, vol. 33, pp. 20673–20684, 2020.
9. T. Guo, S. Guo, J. Zhang, W. Xu, and J. Wang, “Efficient attribute unlearning: Toward selective removal of input attributes from feature representations,” *arXiv preprint arXiv:2202.13295* (2022).
10. J. Hirschberg and C. D. Manning, “Advances in natural language processing,” Science, vol. 349, no. 6245, pp. 261–266, 2015.
11. N. Takahashi, M. Gygli, and L. Van Gool, “Aenet: Learning deep audio features for video analysis,” IEEE Transactions on Multimedia, vol. 20, no. 3, pp. 513–524, 2017.
12. J. Ngiam, A. Khosla, M. Kim, J. Nam, H. Lee, and A. Y. Ng, “Multimodal deep learning,” in Proceedings of the 28th international conference on machine learning (ICML-11), 2011, pp. 689–696.
13. C. Guo, T. Goldstein, A. Hannun, and L. Van Der Maaten, “Certified data removal from machine learning models,” in International conference on machine learning. PMLR, 2020, pp. 3832–3842.
14. S. Ioffe and C. Szegedy, “Batch normalization: Accelerating deep network training by reducing internal covariate shift,” in International conference on machine learning. PMLR, 2015, pp. 448–456.
15. V. Gupta, C. Jung, S. Neel, A. Roth, S. Sharifi-Malvajerdi, and C. Waites, “Adaptive machine unlearning,” Advances in Neural Information Processing Systems, vol. 34, pp. 16 319–16 330, 2021.
16. M. Jagielski, J. Ullman, and A. Oprea, “Auditing differentially private machine learning: How private is private SGD?,” Advances in Neural Information Processing Systems, vol. 33, pp. 22 205–22 216, 2020.
17. B. Jayaraman and D. Evans, “Evaluating differentially private machine learning in practice,” in 28th USENIX security symposium (USENIX Security 19), 2019, pp. 1895–1912.
18. X. Hu, M. Yuan, J. Yao, Y. Deng, L. Chen, Q. Yang, H. Guan, and J. Zeng, “Differential privacy in telco big data platform,” Proceedings of the VLDB Endowment, vol. 8, no. 12, pp. 1692–1703, 2015.
19. C. E. Shannon, “A mathematical theory of communication,” The Bell System Technical Journal, vol. 27, no. 3, pp. 379–423, 1948.
20. A. Thudi, G. Deza, V. Chandrasekaran, and N. Papernot, “Unrolling SGD: Understanding factors influencing machine unlearning,” in 2022 IEEE 7th European symposium on security and privacy (EuroS&P). IEEE, 2022, pp. 303–319.

21. N. Tishby, F. C. Pereira, and W. Bialek, "The information bottleneck method," *arXiv preprint physics/0004057* (2000).
22. C. Molnar, Interpretable machine learning. Lulu.com, 2020.
23. K. Ren, T. Zheng, Z. Qin, and X. Liu, "Adversarial attacks and defenses in deep learning," Engineering, vol. 6, no. 3, pp. 346–360, 2020.
24. M. Veale, R. Binns, and L. Edwards, "Algorithms that remember: Model inversion attacks and data protection law," Philosophical Transactions of the Royal Society A, vol. 376, no, 2133, p. 20180083, 2018.
25. B. Wang, Y. Yao, S. Shan, H. Li, B. Viswanath, H. Zheng, and B. Y. Zhao, "Neural cleanse: Identifying and mitigating backdoor attacks in neural networks," in SP, 2019, pp. 707–723.
26. J. Gao, S. Garg, M. Mahmoody, and P. N. Vasudevan, "Deletion inference, reconstruction, and compliance in machine (Un) learning," Proceedings on Privacy Enhancing Technologies, vol. 3, pp. 415–436, 2022.
27. N. G. Marchant, B. I. P. Rubinstein, and S. Alfeld, "Hard to forget: Poisoning attacks on certified machine unlearning," in AAAI, 2022, pp. 7691–7700.
28. Y. Liu, M. Fan, C. Chen, X. Liu, Z. Ma, L. Wang, and J. Ma, "Backdoor defense with machine unlearning," *arXiv:2201.09538* (2022). https://arxiv.org/abs/2201.09538
29. X. Gao, X. Ma, J. Wang, Y. Sun, B. Li, S. Ji, P. Cheng, and J. Chen, "Verifi: Toward verifiable federated unlearning," IEEE Transactions on Dependable and Secure Computing, vol. 21, no. 6, pp. 5720–5736, 2024.
30. Y. Huang, X. Li, and K. Li, "EMA: Auditing data removal from trained models," in MICCAI, 2021, pp. 793–803.
31. S. Basu, P. Pope, and S. Feizi, "Influence functions in deep learning are fragile," in ICLR, 2021, pp. 1–22.
32. P. W. Koh and P. Liang, "Understanding black-box predictions via influence functions," in ICML, 2017, pp. 1885–1894.
33. Y. Cao, A. F. Yu, A. Aday, E. Stahl, J. Merwine, and J. Yang, "Efficient repair of polluted machine learning systems via causal unlearning," in ASIACCS, 2017, pp. 735–747.
34. R. Guo, L. Cheng, J. Li, P. R. Hahn, and H. Liu, "A survey of learning causality with data: Problems and methods," ACM Computing Surveys, vol. 53, no. 4, pp. 1–37, 2020.
35. T. Eisenhofer, D. Riepel, V. Chandrasekaran, E. Ghosh, O. Ohrimenko, and N. Papernot, "Verifiable and provably secure machine unlearning," *arXiv:2210.09126* (2022). https://arxiv.org/abs/2210.09126
36. Y. Guo, Y. Zhao, S. Hou, C. Wang, and X. Jia, "Verifying in the dark: Verifiable machine unlearning by using invisible backdoor triggers," IEEE Transactions on Information Forensics and Security, vol. 19, no. 1, pp. 708–721, 2023.
37. D. M. Sommer, L. Song, S. Wagh, and P. Mittal, "Athena: Probabilistic verification of machine unlearning," Proceedings on Privacy Enhancing Technologies, vol. 3, pp. 268–290, 2022.
38. J. Weng, S. Yao, Y. Du, J. Huang, J. Weng, and C. Wang, "Proof of unlearning: Definitions and instantiation," IEEE Transactions on Information Forensics and Security, vol. 19, no. 1, pp. 3309–3323, 2024.

Index

For Product Safety Concerns and Information please contact our EU
representative GPSR@taylorandfrancis.com
Taylor & Francis Verlag GmbH, Kaufingerstraße 24, 80331 München, Germany

www.ingramcontent.com/pod-product-compliance
Ingram Content Group UK Ltd.
Pitfield, Milton Keynes, MK11 3LW, UK
UKHW021508240926
475702UK00035B/666

* 9 7 8 1 0 4 1 2 9 5 3 1 0 *